The Gifts of God

The Gifts of God

Eugene V. N. Goetchius

Charles P. Price

MOREHOUSE BARLOW
Wilton, Connecticut

Morehouse Barlow Co., Inc.
78 Danbury Road
Wilton, Connecticut 06897

ISBN 0-8192-1349-7

Library of Congress Catalog Card Number 84-60627

Composition by The Publishing Nexus Incorporated
1200 Boston Post Road, Guilford, Connecticut 06437

Printed in the United States of America

CONTENTS

4

THE GIFTS OF GOD IN THE NEW CREATION: PART TWO

5

USING THE GIFTS: MINISTRY AND MISSION

Acknowledgments

This book was written under the aegis of the Evangelism Ministries of the Education for Mission and Ministry Unit of the Episcopal Church Center. The authors gratefully acknowledge the complaisant assistance of the editorial committee, the members of which were the Rev. Dr. Arlin Rothauge, of the Episcopal Church Center, and Dr. Fredrica Harris Thompsett, Professor of Church history in the Episcopal Divinity School and former Executive Director of the Board for Theological Education. Special thanks are also due to the Rt. Rev. James Michael Mark Dyer, Bishop Coadjutor of Bethlehem, and the Rt. Rev. Elliot L. Sorge, now Bishop of Easton, who read an earlier version of the manuscript and made a number of valuable suggestions which the authors have incorporated. Above all the authors wish to express their appreciation to the Rev. A. Wayne Schwab, Executive Council Staff Officer for Evangelism and Renewal, who by unflagging interest and generous encouragement shared with them his own *charismata* of optimism and enthusiasm.

E.V.N.G.

C.P.P.

1

THE CHURCH MOVES TOWARD RENEWAL

We live in rapidly changing times that challenge the Church in every aspect of its existence. Everywhere the Church faces plausible and powerful rivals that present alternative interpretations of the meaning of human existence and alternative recommendations for ways to live. Old religions speak with new aggressiveness, and secular forms of thought with no room for God present themselves in many attractive variations—from high idealism to pure pleasure-seeking. What is the Church called to do in this situation? This book is written in the conviction that God has a purpose for the Church in this world and that God through the Spirit empowers men and women to accomplish that purpose. We need to open our eyes to see the gifts of God available to us "for the living of these days." This is a book about "the gifts of God for the people of God."

CURRENTS OF RENEWAL

It is no time for business as usual. New strength and new vision are called for—a new sense of the presence of God and of God's power to transform human lives, the Church, and the world. It might be possible to write an entire history of the Church in terms of its continuing renewal by the Spirit from the time when Paul discovered that the congregation in Antioch was making second-class citizens of its Gentile members and, to correct the situation, had to oppose Peter to his face (Gal 2:11ff).[1] It is certainly true that in the twentieth century the Church has sought new ways to meet its new situations. The ecumenical movement represents the quest for one Church, for, as Bishop Brent remarked years ago, "The world is too strong for a divided Church."[2] The liturgical movement represents a quest for honesty and authenticity in worship. Without worship open to the Spirit the Church is impotent. The charismatic revival in its many different manifestations represents the Church opening itself consciously to the many different operations of the Holy Spirit within it.

In the same vein, we might point to the new understanding of the role of the laity in the Church: that "ministry" does not mean only, or even chiefly, the activity of ordained persons on behalf of lay people but much more the activity of lay men and women in the name of Christ on behalf of one another and of those outside the Church. We might point to the new emphasis on Baptism as representing the "ordination of the laity" to this wider ministry of Christ. We should mention the new emphasis on education, particularly adult education, as a significant part of preparing Church members for this ministry. We would include in this inventory of evidence for renewal the new emphasis on evangelism—the effort to communicate the truth about God's love for the world and all the people in it. And we would add a note about the new accent in much theological writing about liberation.[3] "For freedom Christ has set us free" (Gal 5:1). This freedom is increasingly understood to mean freedom not only from those "last enemies" to be destroyed—sin and death—but from political tyranny and psychological bondage as well.

We cannot, however, examine all these currents of renewal in the Church. To do so would take a book in itself. Our purpose is to examine some of the ways the Holy Spirit operates through the spirits of men and women to enable them to play their part in this renewal of the Church that is going on before our eyes. We propose (1) to examine some of the gifts of the Spirit that we encounter in the renewal of the Church and (2) to consider the role of the Spirit as the Giver of gifts.

SOME DEFINITIONS

We need to begin with definitions of basic terms and agreements about the way certain words and phrases will be used.

First we must look at the word *gift* itself. In the New Testament the phrase "spiritual gifts" (*charismata*) has a special meaning and is used in a special way, almost exclusively in the letters of St. Paul. We shall, of course, pay careful attention to these gifts. They constitute a major part of our concern.[4] In normal speech, however, the word "gift" has a much broader range of meaning. Webster's Dictionary gives three definitions: "1: notable capacity or talent; 2: something voluntarily transferred from one person to another without compensation; 3: the act, or power of giving." Even if we limit our consideration to the first area, as we shall, we face all the inherent resources that a person brings to daily living. The dictionary goes on to remind us of the synonyms for gift: "faculty, aptitude, bent, talent, genius, knack." Philo, a Hellenistic Jewish philosopher and older contemporary of St. Paul, spoke of seeing hearing, and reason as "natural gifts."[5] Over and above such capacities, more specific abilities like the capacity to express one's self clearly, to play tennis, or to do carpentry, would naturally be called gifts.

In this book we will use the word "gift" to cover innate and inherent gifts like these, and also what we shall call by way of contrast extraordinary gifts, the *charismata*. Charismata are gifts like the working of miracles, healings, speaking in tongues, the other things listed in the various New Testament lists, and perhaps others. If these latter things are the gifts of God, surely the former are also. To whom else could we attribute them? There are, of course, differences between these two kinds of gifts. The first group is innate or inherent, as we have said. A person is born with the ability to see and hear, and probably also with the ability to play the piano or to do mathematics. Some of these gifts may be possessed in a greater or less degree; some can be developed and improved by practice. But few if any of them ever appear to break in upon a person suddenly from the outside. Gifts in the second group are astonishing and unexpected. Their possessors frequently regard them as manifestations of supernatural power. Most of them are occasional or transitory: they come and go independently of our will. They are beyond the control of the person who has been given them. We shall speak then of innate or inherent gifts as gifts of the Spirit in creation, and of extraordinary gifts as gifts of the Spirit in the Church and for the Church. All are gifts of God.[6]

VARIETIES OF GIFTS

The significance of these two kinds of gifts is at present brought to the attention of the Church by different groups of people. A number of people have been interested in psychology and the power of psychological insight for illuminating and improving human life—the "human potential" movement. They have fastened their attention on the inherent gifts of a person, how they can be identified, understood, accepted, and used for the fulfillment of the individual who possesses them and the well-being of the groups to which the individual belongs.

Bernard Haldane, a well-known exponent of this point of view, writes, for example,

> There is excellence in each person. Its elements are always developing and growing. They start in early childhood and continue throughout life. The elements of a person's excellence are called gifts, skills, traits, talents, strengths, personality factors; and they usually develop in particular environments.[7]

Charismatic renewal movements, on the other hand, are usually more interested in the classical New Testament charismata, the gifts of the Spirit as St. Paul described them, in the Church and for the Church. To be sure, the charismatic movement is broad. It covers many shades of opinion and experience. In its broadest sense, the word charismatic refers to any person or group with a profound and conscious awareness of the gracious presence of God. If the Church lived up to its claims, it would itself be a charismatic movement.

But the Church does not always live up to its claims. It always has to be renewed, as we have seen. And if the ecumenical movement refers to the quest for the renewed unity of the Church and the liturgical movement to the quest for new authenticity in worship, the charismatic movement refers to those aspects of church renewal where the presence and power of God are newly experienced and acknowledged.

The locus of such renewal is usually in local parishes, even in individual members or small groups of members in local parishes. This form of renewal aims to transform the hearts and minds of individual Christians. It may take the form of Bible-study groups, or Encounter Weekends, or participation in the Cursillo movement.

In these manifestations of charismatic renewal, the gifts of the Spirit occasionally include the gift of speaking in tongues, or glossolalia. For some parts of the charismatic revival, however, the gifts of tongues is the most important gift. Christians for whom this gift is essential point for support to the experience of the very first Christians, as recorded in the Acts of the Apostles, beginning with the eleven apostles on the first Christian Pentecost, who "were all filled with the Holy Spirit and began to speak in tongues as the Spirit gave them utterance" (Acts 2:4).

In this book we propose to use the term charismatic in the broader sense described at the beginning of this section. Following W. J. Hollenweger, in his book *The Pentecostals* (Augsburg, 1972), we shall use the term *Neo-Pentecostal* to refer to present-day Christians for whom speaking in tongues is primary and indispensable. We shall examine this gift of tongues in greater detail in a later section.[8]

It is unfortunate, though perhaps understandable and even inevitable, that tension should arise among the people and groups oriented around these two kinds of gifts. Neo-Pentecostals sometimes refuse to recognize as Christian anyone who has not had the kind of experience of the Spirit that produces speaking in tongues. On the other hand, interest in psychology and the innate endowments of human beings has led some of the "human potential" advocates to impatience with theology and to rejection of traditional theological categories.

As the need for the renewal of the Church has grown, however, and contact among the various renewal movements has developed, possibilities for the mutual enrichment of all parties have emerged. This is surely preferable to continued hostility and mistrust.

Perhaps the chief unifying force at work is the ministry of the laity. The service of the world in God's name requires all the gifts the Spirit gives—inherent and extraordinary, in creation and in the new creation. It takes the patience of laboratory researchers and the skill of physicians. It takes the gift of hospitality in open and welcoming communities and the gift of preaching in a pulpit. It takes artists and musicians and poets as well as prophets and sages. It takes imagination and faithfulness, love for God and love for the world God has made. God has bestowed an indescribable profusion of gifts upon us, in unsuspected amounts and combinations. We must learn to recognize them all and use them all for the accomplishment of God's purposes in the world.

2

THE GIFTS OF GOD
IN CREATION

CREATION AS GIFT

God created the world and all that is in it. The Bible begins with this affirmation: "In the beginning God created the heavens and the earth" (Gen 1:1). The Gospel according to St. John reasserts this belief and makes explicit what is implicit in the rest of the New Testament, adding to the teaching that God has created the world the understanding that the agent of creation is the Word of God, which became incarnate in Jesus Christ:

> In the beginning was the Word, and the Word was with God, and the Word was God. He was in the beginning with God; all things were made through him, and without him was not anything made that was made.
>
> (Jn 1:1-3)

Both The Apostles' Creed and the Nicene Creed, the two creeds used in the regular services in the *Book of Common Prayer*, likewise begin by affirming the creative activity of God; "creator of heaven and earth" (*BCP*, p. 96); "maker of heaven and earth, of all that is, seen and unseen" (*BCP*, p. 326). It is a basic and characteristic element of Christian faith.

As God created it, the world was good, indeed "very good" (Gen 1:31). The created order, in spite of its finiteness and materiality, and in spite of the fact that all the finite things in it are impermanent and subject to change and decay, is nevertheless essentailly good. This conviction is a hallmark of

Biblical religion and differentiates Biblical religion from most of the other religions of the world. The world is not *maya*, or illusion, a the Hindu tradition understands it, nor is it the bungled work of an inept craftsman, a deity of lesser rank than the Supreme Being, as Greek philosophy and Gnostic religion held. It is the self-expression of God himself, distinct from him though completely under his control. This conviction makes the existence of evil a major problem. It cannot be accounted for by the intractability of matter—its resistance to the will and purpose of God. But Christians have regularly chosen to face this difficulty rather than to surrender their belief in the goodness of creation.

To regard one's inherent abilities and talents as gifts of God is simply another way of saying that God created them or that God created us with them. This way of looking at our innate endowments—and even that word implies gift!—is frequently encountered in the Old Testament. Several Psalms contain forthright expressions of the idea that our senses are God's workmanship:

> He that planted the ear, does he not hear?
> He that formed the eye, does he not see?
>
> (Ps 94:9)

The Psalmist says to the Lord,

> . . . you yourself created my inmost parts; you knit me together in my mother's womb.
>
> (Ps 139:13)

Not only physical faculties are understood as gifts. The capacity for political leadership, artistic creation, and religious insight are also understood in this way. After the death of Moses, Joshua received from the Lord's hand strength and courage to lead his people (Josh 1:9). Gideon's leadership of the Israelite army against the Midianites and Amalekites was inspired by the Spirit (Jgs 6:34); and, in the course of the erection of the Tent of Witness in the wilderness, the Lord filled Bezalel the son of Uri with the Spirit of God, conferring on his "ability and intelligence, knowledge and all craftsmanship" for making the beautiful things that were to adorn the tent (Ex 31:3).

In a familiar story we learn, in the same vein, that God asked Solomon in a dream, "What shall I give you?" And Solomon replied, "Give your servant therefore an understanding mind to govern your people, that I may discern between good and evil" (1 Kgs 3:9). And in a passage taken to be a description of the hoped-for Messiah of Israel, the prophet Isaiah declared,

> And the Spirit of the Lord shall rest upon him,
> the spirit of wisdom and understanding,
> the spirit of counsel and might,
> the spirit of knowledge and the fear of the Lord.
> And his delight shall be in the fear of the Lord.

> (Isa 11:2f)

This list of gifts is particularly interesting for our purposes, because it is the source of the gifts that the celebrant at Baptism invokes on each newly baptized person, the so-called "seven-fold gift of the Spirit." (The seventh gift, piety [*pietas*], is mentioned only in the Vulgate.[1]) "Give them an inquiring and discerning heart, the courage to will and to persevere, a spirit to know and love you, and the gift of joy and wonder in all your works"(*BCP*, p. 308).

It can be fairly said that the Biblical view of human beings attributes all our abilities, capacities, talents, and skills to the gift of the gracious God who created us. "From the primal elements you brought forth the human race, and blessed us with memory, reason, and skill. You made us rulers of creation . . . " runs one of our Eucharistic prayers (Prayer C, *BCP*, p. 370).

CREATION AND SCIENCE

If we believe that our inherent capacities are gifts of God, does that faith interfere with a scientific investigation of the origin, development, and interrelationship of these gifts with one another and even with the extraordinary "spiritual" gifts called charismata? This book is written in the conviction that there is no conflict between belief in God's creation of the universe and honest scientific inquiry.

Christians believe that God's presence is revealed "at all

times and in all places" and is recognized by God's saving acts. God delivered Israel from the hand of Pharaoh at the Red Sea. This God, Yahweh by name, was the God who created heaven and earth. God delivered Jesus from death itself. Chrtistians know this saving truth by the resurrection of Jesus from the dead, by the forgiveness of their sins, and by the hope of their own resurrection. This God, who frees us from our fears, insecurities, and weaknesses, was the God who created all things through his Son, Jesus Christ. God reveals God's self to us first as our Savior, our deliverer or liberator; then we come to know God as Creator. One does not prove the existence of God by investigating the development of life on earth or by any scientific inquiry. But if we know the power and reality of God to begin with, we may learn about God's ways with his creation by scientific inquiry. As the seventeenth-century astronomer Johannes Kepler wrote, "We do but think God's thoughts after him."

The world with all its creatures and dynamic possibilities comes from the God revealed in Jesus Christ. Everything that exists is grounded and based in God. If the best explanation of how all these things have come to be what they are is the theory of evolution, Christians can gladly accept it. They note, however, the evolution is a *theory*; it is the best hypothesis that the most learned and skilled biologists among us can formulate. It is not an alternative to the Christian doctrine of creation, and it may not be the last word on the subject. If a more plausible explanation should be presented some day, Christians could accept it gladly.

All this is to say that when we claim all our created powers as gifts of God, we do not deny that the study of human beings by biological, psychological, or sociological means will shed light on the subject. We can learn a great deal about our gifts from such studies.

THE GIFT OF FREEDOM

Why should there be anything problematic about the gifts of God? Why should we have to ask about them, study them, analyze them? Yet questions do arise: Why do we have certain gifts, and not others? Why can I remember all the trivia from yesterday's newspaper, while my neighbor on one side can make the best lemon meringue pies in town, my neighbor on the other side can sing like Sills—or Pavarotti, which I'd love to do—and my friend down the block has the knack for repairing gasoline engines, which have always been a complete mystery to me? Why do some people seem to have so many gifts, and others so few? Come to think of it, do I have any gifts at all? Questions like these spring to mind as soon as the topic of God's gifts is mentioned.

Yet, if God has made us, why should there be perplexity and even anxiety about what he has given? "Consider the lilies of the field," Jesus told his disciples in the Sermon on the Mount,

> They neither toil nor spin; yet I tell you, even Solomon in all his glory was not arrayed like one of these. But if God so clothes the grass of the field, which today is alive and tomorrow is thrown into the oven, will he not much more clothe you, O ye of little faith?

> (Mt 6:28-30)

Think for a while in this connection about the difference between lilies of the field and birds of the air on the one hand and human beings on the other. It is an endlessly fascinating question where there is not much certainty. But might it not be suggested that the operative factor in the contrast Jesus drew in the Sermon on the Mount lies in *self-awareness*? Lilies are lilies and birds are birds. As far as we can tell, neither a lily nor a bird is aware of its own identity. A bird perhaps more than a lily: the cardinal singing so beautifully in the holly tree seems to have some sense of its beauty, of how well its plumage shows against the dark green leaves, of how splendid its song is. But neither lily nor bird gives real evidence of interior life; at least, neither is able to communicate that depth of selfhood.

Few other living things, plants or animals, seem to share with human beings the ability to make themselves their own object. A fateful cleavage has occurred in the depths of our human selves: we can look at ourselves as we go about our daily rounds. We can wonder how we are doing. As I write this paragraph I can watch myself write it. I can ask myself about its style, its clarity, its purpose in the design of the chapter. Of course, if I engage in that kind of inner dialogue too long, I shall never get the paragraph written. But is it not also true that if I did not engage in that inner dialogue at all, I should also not get it written? Indeed, perhaps I should not be able to write it at all!

Human beings, we are saying, are self-related. That fact seems to make them different in a significant degree from all other creatures of which we have knowledge. We probably should not claim difference in kind. Birds seem closer to us in this regard than lilies, and other animals, especially pets, seem closer still. Some animals are able to communicate rather abstract kinds of information. Bees, for example, can indicate by a kind of dance the distance and direction of a field of flowers. Nevertheless, such communication falls short of words, and words are the indicators of the deep interior knowledge that is the mark of humanity.

The capacity for self-knowledge and self-expresson is related to a gift we have not yet mentioned—the gift of freedom (cf. 2 Cor 3:17f). Freedom, to be sure, is a word that covers a number of different aspects of the human situation. Basically, it means not belonging to another and is the opposite of slavery. That definition seems to be the original one. In the present context, however, freedom can be understood as the gift of being related to one's self in such a way that one can make one's self an object—an object of study, examination, and comparison; of wonder and even of worry.

In this context the opposite of freedom seems to be *instinct*. Instinct is itself a mysterious quality relating to the harmony of a creature with its environment. The amazing instinctive powers of many insects and higher animals are well-known. Some birds in the course of their migration are apparently so sensitive to the changing length of days, for example, that they arrive at certain points along their course on almost the same day of the year, year after year; and certain species of turtles swim back to the same island year after year in order to spawn. These animals seem to be in tune with, at one with, the realm of nature in a way at which human beings can only marvel. We have lost that close relationship to our environment. We are free.

We are free from our environment and free from ourselves. We are free enough from ourselves to be self-conscious and free enough from our environment not only to sense it through our eyes, ears, and other sensory organs and to know and respond to it in a way presumably comparable to the response of other animals, but also to know it, and to know that we know it. We know ourselves, and we know ourselves in relation to our world. Freedom in this sense is a great gift. It is helpful and suggestive to connect it with our capacity for forming words, for speaking, and therefore for communicating with each other at the level of meaning and feeling. To make one's self one's own object allows one to remember, to compare experiences of today with those of yesterday and last year, to shape concepts, to embrace and express similar experiences, to put ideas into words and to utter them. Freedom in this sense seems closely related to the gift of reason.

Freedom in this sense is also related to the image of God in us. For God, too, we believe, has a similar complexity of being. God, too, we believe, is self-related. At least since the time of St. Augustine, one aspect of the doctrine of the Trinity is the expression of God's inner relations. St. Augustine understood that the affirmation "God is love" implies that there is a way in which God is the lover (the subject), a way in which God is the beloved (the object), and a way in which God is the love that unites subject and object.[2] God, said St. Augustine and a great deal of later Christian theology with him, both knows himself and loves himself. Several verses from the New Testament make the same point. We have already quoted the opening verses of St. John's Gospel: "In the beginning was the Word, and the Word was with God, and the Word was God . . . ." *Word* in this pasage is often taken to denote God as the object of God who is the subject. God knows himself and expresses himself in the Word. In fact, J. B. Phillips' translation of this passage runs, "At the beginning God expressed himself." Both God and God's Word are equally God. Both God as a subject and God as an object are God, much as a human self as subject and a human self as object are equally the human self. The self is the image of God.

The gift of freedom, by which a person can be self-conscious, is the highest of God's gifts that are inherent in human beings, for of all such gifts it is most characteristic of God's being. It is the quality in which our most characteristically human traits are rooted: the capacity for words and reason and the capacity for love.

FREEDOM AND ITS LIABILITIES

Now we must return to the question that started the line of exploration pursued in the previous section. Why should there be anything problematic about the gifts of God? Why should there be perplexity and anxiety about what God has given us? Does not the difficulty arise from freedom as we have tried to describe it, from the mysterious and wonderful gift human beings possess of being self-aware?

The capacity for self-knowledge leads us to recognize in persons a certain doubleness: self as knower, self as known; self as lover, self as beloved. Because of that doubleness we find it necessary to say some rather unusual things about human beings and human growth. We say, for example, that human beings "grow into themselves" or that they "become who they are." "Be yourself," we sometimes say to a friend whose behaviour, we feel, is uncharacteristic. Or we may observe about people with modest gifts who achieve far more than we believed possible, that they have "made the most of themselves." The Prodigal Son "came to himself" (Lk 15:17) before he took his rightful place in his father's house.

In each of these familiar, even colloquial, expressions there is contained an implicit understanding of the self as double. One self, or one aspect of the self, acts. The second aspect of the self is acted upon. One self is subject. The other self is object. But the two aspects of the self are the same self. The subject self "makes something" of the object self. The subject self "becomes" what the object self somehow already is.

It is the purpose of this section to suggest that there are two kinds of problems that arise with the self out of this double structure, two kinds of problems connected with freedom. One kind of problem is related to the limitedness of human beings. The other kind of problem is related to the sheer perversity of human nature. The first are the problems of finitude. The second are the problems of sin. Both affect the gifts of God.

The problems of finitude are problems of growth and development. A baby obviously has little or no sense of himself or herself, no understanding of gifts. Indeed, a child's inherent gifts seldom manifest themselves all at once. Some may evolve slowly, while others may appear rather suddenly. This paragraph is being written in the aftermath of the Washington Redskins' victory at the Superbowl. The hero of the game was John Riggins, whose ability to carry the ball through an apparently impenetrable line of defense dominated the contest. It was said that this extraordinary capacity had emerged only during the last year of his playing, when he began to say in practice, "Give me the ball." And when he carried the ball, he gained yards in an extraordinary way. His gift "burst into view."

Other gifts develop slowly and gradually. Daniel Webster, one of the greatest orators of American politics, said after a moving speech in Congress, "My whole life was a preparation for that speech." His gift evolved.

In either case, the person cannot recognize his or her gift until it flowers. Before the gift develops and before the person in whom it grows sees it and appropriates it, the person is relatively unformed or differently formed. He (or she) "doesn't know who he (or she) is." People whose gifts have not appeared may not think they have gifts. They may wonder why others are more gifted than they. Even after their gift grows, they may not see it or acknowledge it. Self-understanding must grow with the gift.

There is, of course, no fault involved in this situation. No one is to blame. It simply takes time for gifts to develop, and perhaps people need some prompting in order to identify their gifts. Of Jesus himself it was said that he "increased in wisdom and in stature, and in favor with God and man" (Lk 2:52). A virtual scholarly consensus understands that although the New Testament clearly means to say that Jesus was the Messiah from the moment of his conception, he did not begin to understand this gift until his baptism and perhaps did not completely comprehend God's purposes for him until he faced his cross. Such growth in understanding is the stamp of his humanity. All of us—limited, growing, mortal human beings as we are—take time to enter into our gifts. Consequently, we may not understand them fully at any given moment of our life.

Not only do gifts grow, so that it takes time for them to develop. It is also simply the case that finite, mortal men and women are limited. Each has only a few gifts. Some people apparently have more than others, but no one, except God alone, has every gift. No one but God is omnicompetent and omnipotent. It is one of the abiding mysteries of human existence that gifts are so variously distributed in creation, but it is a simple and unavoidable truth. It should perhaps make us realize how much we need each other.

There is no fault involved in this situation, either. No one is to blame. Because of our freedom—freedom in the sense we have tried to establish earlier in this chapter—we can be aware of our own gifts and compare them to the gifts of others. It may be doubted whether other creatures, without this freedom, are able to make such comparisons. In comparing gifts, we may wonder why we have been selected to receive certain ones and not others, and out of that wonder we may learn to give thanks to God because we are so wonderfully made. But we may also find that we are envious because we have not received certain gifts. Envy, however, is part of anxiety and not wonder. We must consider it in the next section.

FREEDOM AND ANXIETY

There is, in fact, a whole other dimension of the problem of gifts. In addition to the set of problems to which our finitude gives rise (problems of wonder and perplexity), there is also the set of problems to which sin gives rise—problems of anxiety, rejection, and distortion.

The Biblical understanding of sin is rooted in freedom. Human beings are free: free from themselves; free to make themselves their own object; free from their environment, so that they are related to the world around them more by decision and deliberation than by instinct; and also free from God, so that they are related to God not by necessity but by free choice. As the opening chapters of Genesis describe the relation between God and his human creatures, he gave them complete freedom from him except for one restriction: they were not to eat of the tree "of the knowledge of good and evil." They were free to obey or disobey that command.

For our purpose we do not need to explore further the meaning of that primal commandment. We simply need to recall that at the very beginning of the Biblical story we find an act of disobedience to God. Human beings are related to God in freedom—the freedom to obey or disobey. They elect disobedience. The rest of the human story is the result of that rebellion. Its name is sin.

It cannot be said too often that in the Bible sin is basically a description of the broken relationship between God and the world, especially between God and humankind. Sin sunders the relationship between God and the sinner. A fundamental insight of Christian faith is that human beings have broken their relation to God and that God seeks to restore it. In Jesus Christ the relationship has been restored.

Our broken relation to God has consequences for all our other relationships. The curse God puts upon Adam and Eve who stand for and represent all human beings—traces the estrangement in the relationship between husband and wife ("Your desire shall be for your husband and he shall rule over you"—Gen 3:16), between mother and child ("I will greatly multiply your pain in childbearing"—Gen 3:16), between worker and work ("In the sweat of your face you shall eat bread"—Gen 3:19). The story of Cain and Abel describes the estrangement of brothers (Gen 4). The story of the Tower of Babel describes the estrangement of nations (Gen 11). These primordial stories about the human condition set the stage for

the call of Abraham (Gen 12) and the history of God's reconciliation of Abraham's children, which by grace we all are. As
Pope Pius XII declared, "Spiritually we are all Semites."

Apart from St. Paul (in Rom 7:14-23), the Biblical authors
pay little attention to the estrangement of the self from the self.
This dimension of sin, to be sure, was not unnoticed during
earlier Christian centuries. But it was not until the nineteenth
century that the Danish philosopher and theologian Søren
Kierkegaard began to explore the inner relations of the self. In
his book *The Sickness Unto Death*[3] he describes a succession of
types of anxiety, a series of different kinds of inner estrangement. Some people are so preoccupied with what might be that
they never commit themselves to any actual goal; some are so
preoccupied with actualities and necessities that they lose all
vision of what might be. Some are so in love with themselves
that they lose the possibility of happy relations with others;
some have such a low opinion of themselves that they do not
dare have relationships with others. The list of ways of being
badly related to one's self goes on and on; it is nearly endless.

What does this analysis of sin have to do with our gifts? Just
this: a distorted relationship to ourselves prevents us from
seeing our gifts accurately and appreciating them realistically.
We may "think of ourselves more highly than we ought to
think" (Rom 12:3) and so set such an overblown value on our
own gifts that we alienate others and cannot use our gifts for
the common good as they are intended to be used. On the
other hand, it is just as serious if we do not accept ourselves or
like ourselves and so reject our gifts and undervalue them.
Then we are not moved to use them or develop them at all.

Nor is our own evaluation of our gifts the only factor at work.
The society we live in places a premium on certain gifts and
disparages others. That is the mark of sin at the local level. Our
society, at least, appears to value aggressiveness,
acquisitiveness, and pragmatic realism. People whose gifts lie
in the direction of gentleness, openness, and theoretical inter-
ests are sometimes thrust aside and undervalued. Such a list is,
of course, by no means complete, and it obviously allows
many exceptions. It is intended simply to suggest some specific ways the pressure to social conformity may incline people

to underrate or overlook the genuine gifts with which God has endowed them. By the same process we become envious of others who seem to have more acceptable gifts. If our finitude leads us to wonder about our gifts, sin makes us anxious about them.

In this situation the Christian gospel comes as good news. It empowers us to accept ourselves as we are—as creatures endowed with some gifts and not with others; as sinners, yet forgiven sinners whom God loves just as we are. And in the Church of Christ still more gifts are given. We must turn, then, to a consideration of the gifts of God in the Church.

3

THE GIFTS OF GOD IN THE NEW CREATION

Part One: The New Testament and the Early Church

Much of the previous chapter dealt with human freedom, which was described as the highest of God's gifts inherent in human beings—indeed, as the gift without which we would not be fully human. We saw how this freedom is essentially related to the image of God in us and how our sinful abuse and misuse of this freedom has resulted in the disfigurement of that image, if not in its total loss.[1] In the present chapter we shall see how God uses his own sovereign freedom to release us from the power of sin and to restore and redeem our human freedom. For when sin vitiated our inherent gifts, God responded with a new outpouring of his Holy Spirit, with new, extraordinary gifts. Since, as we shall see, these extraordinary gifts include or entail the forgiveness of sins, we receive together with them all the "old" innate, inherent gifts—rehabilitated, as it were, and refined for the use God intends us to make of them.

We now turn, therefore, to the New Testament, from which we shall learn how God poured our his Spirit on the earliest Christians, raising them out of confusion and superstition to be a new people of God, a new Israel, even as he had raised his Son Jesus from the dead, empowering them with special gifts to equip them "for the work of ministry, for building up the body of Christ." (Eph 4:12)

What are these special gifts? There are several words in the Greek New Testament that may be translated "gift." The one upon which we shall fix our attention is *charisma*, which has, fortunately or unfortunately, become part of our popular English vocabulary as a name for the special quality possessed by some persons who move rapidly into positions of leadership and gain the unquestioned devotion of large numbers of people. This popular understanding of charisma, however, is remote from that which has been current for many years in Christian Pentecostal circles and which is becoming increasingly familiar in the so-called main-line churches.

In the New Testament,*charisma* (plural *charismata*) occurs almost exclusively in the writings of St. Paul[2] who uses it for a particular kind of gift—a gift sometimes described as "of God' (Rom 6:23; 11:29; 1 Cor 7:7), sometimes as "of the Holy Spirit" (1 Cor 12:4,8). Translators sometimes try to indicate the special nature of charisma by adding qualifying adjectives. Thus *RSV* has "free gift" in Rom 5:15f (twice) and Rom 6:23, "special gift" in 1 Cor 7:7, and "spiritual gift" in 1 Cor 1:7, although these modifiers are not represented separately in the Greek.[3] Paul occasionally uses other words to refer to these same "spiritual" gifts (in Rom 5:15-17 *dorea*, *dorema*, and *charisma* are synonyms), but these are less specialized than charisma and are also used in the New Testament to refer to less exalted, even material "gifts" (Mt 2:11; Lk 21:1, 4; Rev 11:10).

Etymologically related to charisma is *charis*, a word of broader application and fundamental to an understanding of St. Paul. This word, usually rendered in English by "grace"[4] means, for St. Paul, the wholly unmerited favor of God, actualized in the cross of Jesus Christ. Charis, grace, is possessed by every Christian (1 Cor 1:4), and is the basis of salvation (Rom 3:24f; 5:20f; cf. Eph 2:8). The element of God's perfect freedom in giving is fundamental (Rom 3:24f; cf. 4:1-6; 5:15, 17).[5] For Paul, "the whole of life is . . . an expession of grace: all is of grace, and grace is all."[6] He does, however, lay special stress on several particular manifestations of grace, and these he calls charismata.

It is sometimes maintained that these charismata are "supernatural" gifts, not to be confused with natural human talents and abilities.[7] But Paul himself does not make this distinction: for although he nowhere explicitly refers to human talents and abilities as gifts of God, he obviously would not assign them to any other source. Indeed, he writes to the Corinthians,

> What have you that you did not receive? If you then received it, why do you boast as if it were not a gift?
>
> (1 Cor 4:7)

Therefore, though we shall give special attention in this chapter to the extraordinary gifts Paul calls charismata, we do not intend to imply that there is any sharp division between them and the more familiar gifts we call talents, abilities, skills, aptitudes, and faculties; all of these are also given by God, and all are available, valuable, and indispensable for "the work of ministry, for building up the body of Christ" (Eph 4:12).[8]

Various classifications have been suggested for the Pauline charismata,[9] but none has found general acceptance. Certainly Paul himself was not concerned with providing a systematic classification. He was writing to a particular situation in Corinth and, later, to a situation in Rome that he may have had reason to suspect was similar. It will be convenient to begin our discussion by setting forth the four major lists of charismata found in the undisputed Pauline epistles; a very literal translation is given, and the items are assigned letters and numbers for easy reference:

List A: 1 Cor 12:8—10
A1. utterance of wisdom
A2. utterance of knowledge
A3. faith
A4. gifts of healings
A5. working of miracles
A6. prophecy
A7. discernments of spirits
A8. kinds of tongues
A9. interpretation of tongues

List B: 1 Cor 12:28
B1. apostles
B2. prophets

B3. teachers
B4. miracles
B5. gifts of healings
B6. acts of helping
B7. acts of guiding
B8. kinds of tongues

List C: 1 Cor 12:29—30
C1. apostles
C2. prophets
C3. teachers
C4. miracles
C5. gifts of healings
C6. tongues
C7. interpret

List D: Rom 12:6—8
D1. prophecy
D2. service (or ministry)
D3. the one who teaches
D4. the one who exhorts
D5. the one who shares
D6. the one who presides
D7. the one who shows mercy

Apart from these lists Paul uses the term charisma in the following passages:

E. Rom 1:11—I long to see you, that I may share with you some spiritual gift to strengthen you. [No particular charisma is mentioned here, but the passage is important because it tells us that some charismata, at least, can be shared.]

F. Rom 5:15f—But the free gift [charisma] is not like the trespass. For if many died through one man's trespass, much more have the grace of God and the free gift [dorea] in the grace of that one man Jesus Christ abounded for many. And the free gift [dorema] is not like the effect of that one man's sin. For the judgment following one trespass brought condemnation, but the free gift [charisma] following many trespasses brings justification. [The "free gift" here is the saving act of Jesus Christ with all its effects.][10]

G. Rom 6:23—The wages of sin is death, but the free gift of God is eternal life in Christ Jesus our Lord.

H. Rom 11:29—The gifts and the call of God are irrevocable. [Paul refers here to the gifts or privileges granted to Israel, which he has mentioned in Rom 9:4f—sonship, glory, the covenants, the giving of the law, worship, the promises, the patriarchs, and the Messiah.]

I. 1 Cor. 1:7—. . . so that you are not lacking in any spiritual gift. [Paul gives thanks that the Corinthians have been enriched in Christ with all speech and knowledge, with this result.]

J. 1 Cor 7:7—I wish that all were as I myself am [i.e., unmarried]. But each has his own special gift from God. [Paul regards his ability to remain celibate as a charisma.]

K. 1 Cor 12:31—But earnestly desire the higher gifts. (Cf. *infra*, p. 35.)

L. 2 Cor 1:11—You must also help us by prayer, so that many will give thanks on our behalf for the blessing (*charisma*) granted to us.[Some commentators think this charisma is God's "gracious intervention" to deliver Paul from danger, But Conzelmann holds that it means "the totality of the conferred gift of salvation."[11]]

Even a casual reading of the four lists suggests that Paul had not carefully considered his terminology, to say the least. In no one of the lists are all the items really coordinate; this awkwardness of style (obscured in most English translation) is doubtless due—at least in the Corinthian lists—to the fact that Paul is addressing special circumstances while at the same time trying to incorporate traditional material. Thus the mention of "utterance of wisdom" and "utterance of knowledge" is in response to the Corinthians' boasting (cf. 1 Cor 1:17, 19-31; 2:1-5, 18-20; 8:1-3), as are the repeated references to speaking in tongues; the triad of "offices"—apostles, prophets, and teachers, explicitly enumerated as "first . . . second . . . third . . . "—

on the other hand, is probably traditional, being included by way of defending Paul's own authority.[12] The list in Romans has fewer infelicities of style, but is characterized by a vagueness we might expect in a letter written to a community with which Paul was less familiar.

In sorting out the items in these lists for discussion we find the most obvious division is between those that denote persons (B1, B2, B3 = C1, C2, C3, D3, D4, D5, D6, D7) and those that refer to functions or activities (A1, A2, A4 = B5 = C5, A5 = B4 = C4, A6 = D1, A7, A8 = B8 = C6, A9 = C7, B6, B7, D2). The term *faith* (A3), however, falls into neither group. Let us consider faith first.

THE CHARISMA OF FAITH

Faith is certainly not on the same level as "utterance of wisdom," "gifts of healings," "discernments of spirits," and so on, though Paul treats it as parallel to these in 1 Cor 12:8—10. But it is only in this list that Paul calls faith a charisma; elsewhere (Gal 5:22) he calls it a "fruit" of the Spirit. In any case we can hardly suppose that Paul thought of faith as one gift among many, since he makes it a prerequisite for the working of miracles (1 Cor 13:2), speaks of prophecy "in proportion to" faith (Rom 12:6), and associates faith with God's graciousness—hence, by implication, with all charismata—as a measure or standard (Rom 12:3).

It is essential to bear in mind that faith, in the new Testament, never means uncritical belief or credulity. Indeed, the Greek word for faith (*pistis*) also means *faithfulness*. For this reason St. Paul is able to use faith to refer to the fundamental relationship between God and human beings that is the basis of our salvation and has been actualized by Christ's reconciling work.[13]. It is God's faithfulness, revealed in Jesus Christ, that calls forth our faith—which is ours because it is a charisma, a free gift.[14] Faith is rather an "all-purpose" gift, like the charismata of salvation (cf. *supra* F: Rom 5:15f, and L: 2 Cor 1:11) and eternal life (G: Rom 6:23), which are intimately related to it. These charismata are the basic equipment needed by every

Christian for every form of ministry. These are the extraordinary gifts that redeem and renew the gift of freedom, which is inherent in human beings but which has been sinfully misused by them. Possessing these gifts, Christians are set free from bondage to sin, set free from depression and indecision, set free from selfish concern and anxiety—set free for confident action for building up the body of Christ. It was the possession of these gifts that made it possible for St. Paul to say, "I can do all things through Christ, who strengthens me" (Phil 4:13). God's Holy Spirit guarantees the same gifts to us, today (2 Cor 5:5).

Returning now to Paul's four lists, let us consider the terms that refer to functions or activities. These may be subdivided into those having to do with speech or utterance and those having to do with acts of service.

CHARISMATA OF UTTERANCE

Utterance of Wisdom and Knowledge

"Utterance of wisdom" and "utterance of knowledge" are mentioned as separate charismata (1 Cor 12:8), but it is not easy to draw a distinction between them.[15] Important to notice here is that, for Paul, neither wisdom nor knowledge is a gift: what the Spirit imparts is the power of communicating wisdom or knowledge to others.[16] Paul disparages the notions of wisdom and knowledge so dear to the hearts of the "spiritual" Corinthians. Their worldly wisdom, he says, is mere foolishness with God (1 Cor 3:19; cf. 1:20-25), while their knowledge "puffs up" (1 Cor 8:1) and may cause less knowledgeable Christians to stumble (1 Cor 8:11). In place of the "wisdom of this world" Paul proclaims the wisdom of God and the power of God, which is Jesus Christ (1 Cor 1:24); spurning theoretical knowledge, Paul determined to know nothing except Jesus Christ crucified (1 Cor 2:2). What Paul condemns in the early chapters of 1 Corinthians is not, however, speculative wisdom and theoretical knowledge in general, but only as these are put forward as means to salvation available only to a privileged few (cf. 1 Cor 1:21). What is at issue here is the incipient Gnosticism of the Corinthians, not some kind of anti-intellectualism on the part of Paul.[17]

For Christian faith, secular wisdom and knowledge are matters indifferent (*adiaphora*): many brilliant philosophers and scientists have not been Christians, but many others equally brilliant have devoted their wisdom and knowledge to the service of Christ and his Church. For Christian faith, again, Jesus Christ is the repository of "all the treasures of wisdom and knowledge" (Col 2:3; cf. Rom 11:33—36); these treasures are the "unsearchable riches" (Eph 3:8) proclaimed by those who have received the charismata of "utterance of wisdom" and "utterance of knowledge." For Christian faith, finally, wisdom and knowledge consist first of all in grateful acknowledgment of the mighty acts of God in Jesus Christ, the understanding of which is not a fixed, unchanging possession, but one that grows and deepens in the Christian life of obedience and reflection.[18]

Prophecy and Teaching

The gifts of utterance we have been discussing are obviously related to the gifts of prophecy and teaching, both of which are concerned with communication. Prophecy expresses "a new word from God as such, whereas teaching [expresses] a new insight into an old word from God."[19] Prophecy is the only charisma referred to in all of Paul's lists (A6 = D1, B2 = C2; cf. Eph 4:11). Paul emphasizes that prophecy is the utterance of intelligible words given by the Spirit) cf. 1 Cor 14:28—30); elsewhere in the New Testament, however, as in the Hebrew Scriptures, prophecy is understood to include predictive oracles as well as inspired proclamations.[20] Paul values prophecy above all other charismata (1 Cor 14:1) because it, more than any other, builds up the community of believers in their faith and in their common life and worship. Prophecy builds up because it speaks to particular needs: the need may be for a word of sympathetic encouragement or exhortation (1 Cor 14:3, 31; "exhortation" is called a separate charisma in Rom 12:8 [D4], but surely it is an aspect of prophecy) or a word revealing some spiritual truth (1 Cor 14:6). Prophecy also builds up because it is a "sign for believers" (1 Cor 14:22). To be sure, prophecy can also be a sign for unbelievers: by its inspiration and content prophecy reveals that God is present in the community, able to "lay bare the secrets of the heart" (1 Cor 14:24f).

A Christian exercises the charisma of teaching when he or she expresses some aspect of authoritative tradition in a new way—a way that builds up the Church. Examples of such charismatic teaching can be seen in Paul's use of sayings of Jesus (1 Th 4:2-5; 1 Cor 7:10f; 9:14f), and especially in his treatment of the Old Testament (Rom 11:15ff; 1 Cor 9:8ff; Gal 3:8).

Glossolalia

The most controversial of the charismata of inspired utterance is *glossolalia*, speaking with tongues (1 Cor 12:10, 28, 30; 13:1, 8; 14:2, 4, 5, 6, 9, 13f, 18, 22f, 26f, 39). In this section we shall try to answer three questions: (1) What was Corinthian glossolalia? (2) What did St. Paul think it was? (3) What shall we say about glossolalia today?

We can see and hear the Corinthians only through the eyes and ears of Paul. The picture he gives us of the Corinthian community (in 1 Cor 12:2f; 14:12, 23, 27f, 33, 40) is certainly one of confusion and disorder, but hardly seems to justify Dunn's confident assertion that glossolalia as practiced in Corinth "was a form of ecstatic utterance—sounds, cries, words uttered in a state of spiritual ecstasy."[21] It is clear, however, that Paul regarded the Corinthian tongue-speaking as inspired utterance, for it is with another form of inspired utterance—prophecy—that he contrasts it. Moreover, those who speak, pray, and sing in tongues, Paul tells us, do so "in the Spirit" even though they do not do so "with the mind" (1 Cor 14:2f, 14f). Clearly, then, Paul regarded glossolalia as *mindless* utterance; equally clearly, however, he thought of it as a real language. He refers to "tongues" as *glossai*, which is the ordinary Greek word for languages, and he believes they can be translated. (The word used to designate the charisma of interpretation—*hermeneia*—is the usual Greek word for translation.) Paul does not, however, think of glossolalia as speaking in human foreign languages: he treats it as *analogous* to human foreign languages in 1 Cor 14:10, so it is clear that he does not consider it to be itself merely another human foreign language.[22] He seems rather to have thought of it as the language of heaven (cf. Rev 14:2f) in which one speaks not to human beings, but to God (1 Cor 14:2). Foreign languages are "tongues of men"; glossolalia is "tongues of angels."

Paul does not himself value glossolalia very highly. He relegates it to the bottom of his lists in 1 Cor 12:8-10, 28, and says that he would rather speak five words with his mind than ten thousand words in a tongue (1 Cor 14:19). Nevertheless, he boasts that he speaks in tongues more than all of the Corinthians (1 Cor 14:18). Paul discourages unrestrained use of glossolalia (1 Cor 14:5-12, 19), but, since he recognizes it as a genuine charisma, he allows it a modest place in public worship (1 Cor 14:27f, 39), even though he plainly feels it serves no useful purpose there (1 Cor 14:6-19). Indeed, Paul says that glossolalia is a "sign for unbelievers" (1 Cor 14:22)—a sign "not of their closeness to God but of their distance from God. ..." As glossolalia confirms the unbeliever in his unbelief (v. 23—"You are mad = God is not here), so prophecy confirms the believer in his faith (v. 25: God is here.)"[23]

The main reason for Paul's low valuation of glossolalia is that it does not build up the church: "He who speaks in a tongue edifies himself, but he who prophesies edifies the church" (1 Cor 14:4). Throughout the fourteenth chapter of 1 Corinthians Paul contrasts prophecy with glossolalia. Both, he insists, are forms of inspired utterance—"speaking in the spirit"—but prophecy is also "speaking with the mind." Glossolalia is permissible for one who "speaks not to men but to God" (1 Cor 14:2). As inspired prayer glossolalia "builds up" the tongue-speaker who experiences it as effective communication with God (Rom 8:26-28).

What about glossolalia today? Is it a purely psychological phenomenon—and a pathological one at that? Or is it still a manifestation of a charisma St. Paul recognized even though he tried to "soft-pedal" it? The linguist William J. Samarin, after surveying the major psychological theories that have been put forward in the last century, concludes that "the attempt to explain glossolalia psychologically is not an impressive one."[24] Is it then a true charisma? As Rom 12:6 implies, a charisma is an experience of grace given; if glossolalia is so experienced, there seems to be no reason not to call it a charisma. Certainly there can be little doubt that most, if not all, modern tongue-speakers do feel that they have received an experience of divine grace. In Dunn's understanding of the term, of course, the charisma of glossolalia is the particular utterance, "not a latent power or ability which may be sometimes displayed and sometimes not."[25] Samarin shows, however, that—regardless of the manner in which glossolalia is "acquired"[26]—it may be deliberately cultivated, practiced, and improved like a skill, even as one can, by practice, improve one's ability to speak a natural human language.[27]

For our purposes, however, the important question is not whether glossolalia is a charisma, but whether it is one that is necessary "equipment for the saints for the work of ministry, for the building up of the body of Christ" (Eph 4:12). Paul conceded, in 1 Cor 14:4, that persons who speak in tongues are thereby individually edified. Since a Christian community, like others, is made up of individuals, the edification—the "building up"—of each individual member is important for the whole community. In what ways, then, can we understand this "building up" as happening? In the first place, tongue-speaking has symbolic value for the speakers; it is for them a sign of symbol of their transition from their "old" life to their "new" life.[28] Secondly, tongue-speaking builds up individuals because they find it not only enjoyable but exhilarating.[29] Finally, tongue-speaking edifies the speaker because—for the speaker, though not for others—it has expresssive value. This function of glossolalia is associated with prayer (Rom 8:26f; 1 Cor 14:2). One of Samarin's respondents writes, "As I pray to God in a tongue I receive back from him a clarifying of many things in the conscious mind," and another says, "I pray in tongues and often the answer will come into my mind as if it had been there all the time—when I did not know the answer."[30] In addition to these positive values glossolalia has for individuals, has it any for the congregation? In Pentecostal and Neo-Pentecostal groups glossolalia often has the function of indicating solidarity with the group; this could be considered a positive value were it not that it often has the effect of dividing a community into those who do and those who do not speak with tongues. Any gift can, of course, become the occasion for divisions in a community if it is misused or regarded as the private preserve of an elite group. St. Paul argues against this in his metaphor of the body and its members (1 Cor 12:12—27; Rom 12:4f): all Christians have gifts, but not all have the same gift—and there is no gift the lack of which can exclude one from the body of Christ. If this danger is recognized and avoided, glossolalia can have at least one positive practical function in the congregation: it can contribute to the spontaneity of a meeting. "Because a discourse or utterance in tongues can come unexpectedly at almost any point, it reminds the participants that this is an open meeting"—God is not somehow restricted by the rigid structure of the liturgy. Moreover, as a manifestation of the divine, it may contribute "a sacred note to a meeting... [a pervasive] feeling of awe and keen awareness of the divine presence."[31]

Interpretation of Tongues

The charisma of interpretation is so closely linked in Paul's thought to the charisma of tongues that he will not permit the latter in the assembly unless it is accompanied by the former (1 Cor 14:5, 13, 26—28). In Paul's view, it is only through the accompanying interpretation that glossolalia can benefit the community. He insists on this companion gift in order to ensure that the charisma of glossolalia will be a true charisma: not merely a gift from God, but a gift from God for others. Is the charisma of interpretation still with us? To this question Samarin gives a qualified "yes"; since he holds that a "glossolalic discourse is meaningless (except for affect or feeling)," he understandably concludes that a charismatic "interpretation" cannot somehow be a rendition of it.[32] Even the leaders of Pentecostal and Neo-Pentecostal groups do not maintain that an "interpretation" is a translation of a glossolalic utterance, but only that it is a sort of commentary or explanation. This distinction, Samarin observes, "is based on no linguistic comparison [and] only puts the phenomena beyond reach of critical assessment."[33] Glossolalists themselves, however, generally take interpretation quite seriously; some indeed follow St. Paul in forbidding the public use of tongues unless there is someone to interpret.[34] An obvious "scientific" method for testing the validity of charismatic interpretation would be to compare several interpretations of the same glossolalic discourse; this, however, is not encouraged.[35] The Church's way of testing an interpretation, of course, is the same as that for testing any other gift, namely, by using the communal charisma of discernment or evaluation. Certainly the "cumbersome two-stage gift"[36] of tongues-plus-interpretation seems to be functionally equivalent to a single utterance of prophecy in the language of the community. The interpretation is surely, in Paul's usage, an inspired utterance, but—unlike prophecy—it is in some way dependent on a preceding inspired utterance of glossolalia. What is the nature of this dependence? Paul does not tell us, and it is difficult to see how he can have thought the connection to be a rational one, since it is impossible to conceive of a rational interpretation of a "mindless" (Paul, 1 Cor 14:13f) or "meaningless" (Samarin) utterance, however inspired the latter might be. Perhaps, it may be conjectured, if the two admittedly interdependent charismata are truly present, the exercise of the one "triggers" in some way the exercise of the other, the end result being much the same as that of exercising the single charisma of prophecy. This suggestion finds some support in Dunn's observation that "in the twentieth century Pentecostal and charismatic movements the interpretation of a tongue has often sounded more like a prophecy than the inerpretation of a prayer."[37] There is also something attractive in the notion of a charisma that does not have its full value—or, indeed, any value at all—in the community without a complementary, cooperating charisma. It reminds us that Christians do not, cannot, exercise their ministries apart from one another any more than they can do so apart from Jesus Christ (cf. Mt 18:19f)

CHARISMATA OF SERVICE

In his list of charismata in the twelfth chapter of Romans, Paul puts in second place, between prophecy and teaching, a gift for which the Greek is *diakonia*. This word is usually translated by *ministry* in the King James Version (KJV), but is often changed to *service* in the Revised Standard Version (RSV); in the same way KJV prefers *minister* (noun) to RSV *servant*, and *minister* (verb) to RSV *serve*.[38]

None of these renderings is wholly satisfactory. "Minister" and "ministry" have rather narrowly restricted meanings in modern everyday English. As a noun, "minister" usually means a member of the clergy, a pastor, a person authorized to officiate at religious ceremonies. As a verb, "minister" means to attend to the needs and wants of others: we speak, for example, of the Red Cross "ministering" to people left homeless after a flood. Finally, the word "ministry" usually means the profession of a minister—a minister of religion. We might say that "ministry" and "minister" have become specialized in an upward direction. Many people regard the ministry as simply another profession parallel to those of law and medicine; to many people a minister is a member of that profession, a person in whose presence one should watch one's language.

"Service," "serve," and especially "servant," on the other hand, have been specialized in a downward direction.[39] Most Americans, certainly, feel that serving, being a servant, is beneath their dignity. Most ancient Greeks shared this view, holding that "ruling and not serving is proper to a man."[40] Even Plato believed that the only honorable kind of service was service to the state, and among the Stoics the idea of having concrete obligations toward one's neighbors almost disappears.[41]

The Jews had a very different understanding of service. They found nothing unworthy in serving, especially when they were servants of a great master, and supremely when they rendered service to God.[42]

In the teaching of Jesus both the Greek and Jewish attitudes toward serving are transcended. When Jesus came as Son of man "not to be ministered unto, but to minister" (Mk 10:45

KJV) "not to be served, but to serve" (Mk 10:45 *RSV*; cf. Mt 20:28; Lk 22:26), he completely reversed all previous human valuations of greatness and rank. What was beneath the dignity of the ancient Greeks—and of many modern men and women as well—is for the Christian the only way to greatness; to achieve greatness the Christian must become "servant of all' (Mk 9:35), even "slave of all" (Mk 10:44).

Jesus came "to serve, and to give his life as a ransom for many" (Mk 10:45). Thus the ideal of ministry, of service, that Jesus sets before us includes more than assistance—even loving assistance—rendered to our neighbors: it may include suffering for others, even dying for them, even as Jesus himself did: "Anyone who wishes to enter my service must follow me, and where I am, there also will my servant be; and anyone who serves me will be honored by my Father" (Jn 12:26). Thus it is clear that serving our neighbor, serving Christ, and serving God are one and the same thing. God does not need our service, but he has provided us with neighbors who do—and the reward for such service is fellowship with God.[43]

No one, however, can undertake this service for the sake of gaining this reward, for this service (or ministry) is a charisma bestowed by the Holy Spirit, a task God gives us the opportunity, the ability, the responsibility, and the grace to perform. The ministry par excellence is, of course, the ministry of reconciliation committed to us by God in Jesus Christ (2 Cor 5:18), but this includes many varieties of ministries corresponding to many varieties of charismata (1 Cor 12:4-7). A particular ministry is a charisma whose divine origin is attested by the fact that it serves the needs of others and so builds up the Church. There are many examples of such ministries in the New Testament: Paul's collection for the Church in Jerusalem is so called (Rom 15:31; 2 Cor 8:4; 9:1, 12f), as is the service—presumably hospitality—rendered by Stephanas and his family (1 Cor 16:15). Paul speaks of his own ministry to the Corinthians—for which he received no compensation (2 Cor 11:8)—and refers to the whole of his work as a ministry, a sustained act of service (Rom 11:13, 2 Cor 3:8f; 4:1; 5:18; 6:3). In the Acts of the Apostles we have the preaching of the Gospel described as a ministry or service of the word (Acts 6:4), and the apostolic office itself is described as a ministry or service (Acts 1:17, 25; 20:24). Other charismata mentioned in Rom 12:8 and 1 Cor 12:28 may also be counted as varieties of service or ministry. "Acts of guiding" (B7: *kybernēseis*) in 1 Cor 12:28 must mean those gifts that qualify a Christian to be a helmsman (*kybernētes*) of the community, "a true director of its order and therewith of its life."[44] It follows that these were the gifts possessed by "the one who presides" (D6: *proistamenos*) of Rom 12:8.[45] Similarly, "acts of helping" (B6: *antilēmpseis*) in 1 Cor 12:28 may reasonably be understood to include the charismata of "the one who shares" (D5) and "the one who shows mercy" (D7) mentioned in Rom 12:8.[46] The Greek word for "sharing" (*metadidonai*) can be used of giving a share in a particular charisma (E. Rom 1:11) or in the Gospel (1 Th 2:8), but here it probably means merely the sharing of food and possessions within the community. Those who have the gift to exercise this ministry, Paul says, must do so with simplicity and sincerity (*haplotēti*)—that is, without ulterior motives: "If I give away all that I possess, and if I deliver my body to be burned, but have not love, I gain nothing" (1 Cor 13:3). Sharing that is loveless is also worthless. "The one who shows mercy" (D7) is exhorted to do so "with cheerfulness" (*hilarotēti*). Calvin wisely commented:

> As nothing affords more consolation to the sick or to anyone otherwise distressed than the sight of helpers eagerly and readily disposed to afford him help, so if he observes gloominess in the face of those who help him, he will take it as an affront.[47]

CHARISMATA OF HEALING

Healing is clearly a "variety of service" or ministry, but it is such an important one it seems best to treat it separately. Indeed, to Paul's way of thinking, healing is not itself a single gift. He never speaks of a charisma of healing but always of charismata of healings, using both words in the plural whenever they occur (1 Cor 12:9, 28, 30). Dunn suggests, not unreasonably, that "as there are many (different) illnesses, so there are many (different) healing charismata."[48] Somewhat surprisingly, this same scholar understands "healing" in a very narrow sense, as the cure of (mental or physical) diseases; he devotes a scant fifteen lines to discussing these gifts.[49] There is, however, no reason to limit our understanding of healing in this way, for it was certainly not so limited in the thought-world of the New Testament. To be sure, healing did, then as now, mean the cure of diseases of every sort. Paul's "charismata of healings" surely include "gifts" for curing diseases, and the power Jesus gave his disciples to cast out demons (Mk 3:14f; 6:7) is explicitly stated to include the power to heal sickness (Mt 10:1; Lk 9:1f).

In the ancient world, however, a relationship between sickness and sin was recognized by both pagan and Jewish thinkers. In consequence of this the various words for "heal" came to have more than a strictly medical sense and were applied analogically in other fields, with the broader meanings "restore," "make whole," and even "save."[50] Thus Plato assigns to the lawgiver the task of healing the unlawful pursuit of gain, which is a disease of the soul (*Laws*, IX, 862c), and praises the god of love (Eros) who "restores us to our original nature and by healing makes us blessed and happy" (*Symposium*, 193d).

The Old Testament bears ample witness to the notions of sickness as the result of sin and of the cure of sickness as the result of divine forgiveness:

Return, O faithless sons, and I will heal your faithlessness.
(Jer 3:22)

Heal me, O Lord, and I shall be healed:
    save me and I shall be saved.
(Jer 17:14)

As for me, I said, "O Lord, be gracious to me;
    heal me, for I have sinned against thee!"
(Ps 41:4)

Bless the Lord, O my soul, and forget not all his benefits, who forgives all your iniquity, and heals all your diseases.
(Ps 103:2f)[51]

Thus healing, in its fullest and deepest sense, is nothing less than the forgiveness of sins. Jesus himself makes this equation in replying to his critics after healing the paralytic who had been let down through the roof by his friends (Mt 9:1-8 = Mk 2:1-12 = Lk 5:17-26): "Which is easier, to say, 'Your sins are forgiven,' or to say, 'Rise and walk'?"

The usual Greek verbs for "heal" (in both literal and figurative senses) are *therapeuein* (from which we get *therapy* and *therapeutic*) and *iasthai* (which is the source of the *ia* in *psychiatrist* and *pediatrics*). In the Synoptic stories of healings by Jesus, however, the verb *sōzein* occurs sixteen times. *Sozein* has approximately the meanings of English "save," i.e., preserve, keep from harm, and rescue. In the Synoptic healing narratives it clearly means "save from disease" (as it does, e.g., in the writings of Hippocrates) or "save from demon possession." But, since it can elsewhere mean "save from eternal death, judgment, and sin," we cannot avoid perceiving suggestive overtones—especially in the eight stories that contain the words "Your faith has saved you" (Mk 5:34 and parallels; Mk 10:52 & parr; Lk 7:50; 17:19). English versions translate *sōzein* in these passages as if it meant physical healing only (*KJV*, "hath made thee whole"; *RSV*, "has made you well"; Phillips "has healed you"; *NEB*, "has cured you"), but the choice of the word by the Evangelists at least "leaves room for the view that the healing power of Jesus and the saving power of faith go beyond physical life."[52]

In the writings of St. Paul *sōzein* has only its religious sense, "to save from sin and eternal death." To be saved in this sense means to possess salvation, to be completely and finally healed of the awful disease of sin that infects our race. Healing in this broad sense can also be understood to include justification (being put right with God) and reconciliation (having one's proper relationship to God reestablished). In all these healing activities, however, the initiative remains with God. Just as a physician cannot heal himself (Lk 4:23), no one can justify himself before God (Lk 10:29) nor be reconciled to God by mutual agreement, as a husband and wife might be (1 Cor 7:11). In relation to salvation, justification, and reconciliation God is not on equal terms with human beings: the supremacy of God is always maintained.

> He saved us, not because of deeds done by us in righteousness, but in virtue of his own mercy, by the working of regeneration and renewal in the Holy Spirit which he poured out upon us richly through Jesus Christ our Savior, so that we might be justified by his grace and become heirs in hope of eternal life.
>
> (Tit 3:5-7)

> All this is from God, who through Christ reconciled us to himself and gave us the ministry of reconciliation; that is, in Christ God was reconciling the world to himself, not counting their trespasses against them, and entrusting to us the message of reconciliation.
>
> (2 Cor 5:18f)[53]

By God's grace we have become nothing less than fellow-workers with God (1 Cor 3:9).

CHARISMATA OF OFFICE

At least some of the functions performed by St. Paul and others in the earliest Christian communities were official in nature: that is, they were characterized by such "official" elements as duration, authority, title, legitimation, exceptional position, and compensation—though only very rarely by all these elements at once.[54] No doubt all "official" functions were "charismatic" in a broad sense, inasmuch as those who exercised these functions were, so far as we can tell, entrusted with them because they possessed appropriate abilities or "gifts." In any case, it is frequently difficult to distinguish sharply between charismatic and official functions in the Pauline and other early Christian communities.[55]

The functions exercised by apostles, prophets, and teachers are each characterized by one or more of the "official" elements mentioned above, and the titles themselves have pride of place in two of Paul's lists (B & C: 1 Cor 12:28-30). The fact that all of them were ascribed to Jesus himself may be some indication of the esteem in which they were held.[56] We are justified in calling these offices charismatic because they were established by the activity of the Holy Spirit for building up the Church.

This is obvious in the case of prophets and teachers, who exercised the charismata of prophecy and teaching on a regular basis. There were groups of recognized prophets and teachers at Corinth (1 Cor 12:28f; 14:29ff) and Antioch (Acts 13:1), and doubtless elsewhere (cf. Gal 6:6). There were also prophets, at least, who traveled from place to place (Acts 11:27; 15:32).

Prophets did not derive their authority from a charisma of office. However, it was the charisma of prophecy, regularly exercised, that defined the office. Anyone might prophesy exceptionally or occasionally, and "authority lay in the prophesying and not in the prophet."[57] Whatever the true nature of their authority, however, it is clear that recognized prophets were treated with considerable respect, for at a very early period we find false prophets trying to impose on the credulity and generosity of Christian communities.[58]

Teachers had, or soon came to have, a more "official" character than prophets. This was due to their two-fold responsibility, first, to interpret the tradition, and second, to transmit it. The interpretation of tradition is more obviously charismatic, approaching the charisma of prophecy; but the transmission of tradition is indispensable—particularly in the case of the apostolic preaching (*kērygma*) and the sayings of Jesus. The importance of correct teaching is emphasized again and again (Rom 16:17; 1 Cor 4:17; 11:2; Col 1:28; 2:7; 2 Th 2:15; 3:6). Teachers thus posessed a dual authority: the authority of the tradition itself, and the charismatic authority exercised in interpreting the tradition.[59]

We have postponed the discussion of apostles because their functions and authority include those of both prophets and teachers—and more besides. Paul uses "apostle" in two senses. In 2 Cor 8:23 and Phil 2:25 it means "delegate, envoy"—one having authority to represent his (or her)[60] community elsewhere. In this sense an apostle is obviously the holder of an office and derives his (or her) authority from the office; it is not charismatic authority, however, since the office is bestowed not by Jesus Christ but by the community the apostle represents. In 1 Cor 15:7-9, however, Paul speaks of apostles of Christ: these, rather than the delegates of churches, are the charismatic apostles of 1 Cor 12:28f.

Apostles in this second sense—apostles par excellence—formed a select circle that included only those who (1) had been called and empowered directly by "Jesus Christ and God the Father"—"not by human beings" (Gal 1:1; cf. Rom 1:5; 1 Cor 1:1; 9:1; 15:7f); (2) had been commissioned as missionaries to proclaim the Gospel and to be the founders of churches (Gal 1:15f; Rom 11:13f; 1 Cor 3:5f, 10; 9:2; 2 Cor 4:1, 5); and (3) had suffered for the sake of the Gospel (1 Cor 4:9; 2 Cor 11:23-33; cf. 4:1, 7-12; Gal 6:17.)[61] Moreover, the apostles of Jesus Christ had (4) a decisive eschatological role (Rom 11:13-15; 15:15f; 1 Cor 4:9—"last of all"; 15:8; cf. Eph 3:5): hence there can be no apostles after the original ones.[62]

Paul exercised special authority in Corinth and other communities not because he was an apostle of the "universal Church" but because he was the founder of those communities (1 Cor 4:14f; 2 Cor 10:13-16; 12:14; 1 Th 2:11). This is why he resisted others who claimed apostolic authority in Corinth and derided them as "super-apostles" (2 Cor 11:5; 12:11) and "pseudo-apostles" (2 Cor 11:13).

Paul's authority as an apostle was unquestionably charismatic, since it derived from the call and commission of the risen Christ. This authority was validated, moreover, by the success of his commission in particular communities: those who had experienced his apostolic authority in their conversion were unable to reject it later without denying the genuineness of their own faith (cf. 1 Cor 9:1f; 2 Cor 3:2f; 11:2).

Paul, and doubtless other apostles as well, seems to have exercised all of the charismata. True, he never calls himself a prophet or a teacher, although this is implied in 1 Cor 14:6. He surely spoke as a prophet when he revealed the will of God concerning the salvation of the Jews, whose hearts had been hardened to allow time for the conversion of the Gentiles (Rom 11:25ff), and again when he proclaimed the resurrection and transfiguration of Christians at the parousia (1 Cor 15:23-58; cf. 1 Th 4:13ff). Indeed, all of Paul's letters are filled with prophetic proclamation for building up the Church,[63] and in 1 Cor 4:17 he explicitly says that he teaches.[64]

As an apostle, however, Paul differs from other prophets because his authority is not derived from present (and perhaps only exceptional or transitory) inspiration but from decisive revelatory events in the past. Paul differs from other teachers because his authority is not derived, like theirs, solely from his teaching, but from his unique relationship to the exalted Christ.

Paul describes himself most frequently as a servant or minister (*diakonos*) (1 Cor 3:5; 2 Cor 3:6; 6:4; 11:23) and refers to the many services or ministries he performs (Rom 11:13; 15:31; 1 Cor 3:8f; 4:1; 5:18; 6:3; 8:4; 9:1; 12f; 11:8). He never lays explicit claim to the charismata of healing or miracles, though he alludes to what Christ has wrought through him "by the power of signs and wonders and mighty works" (2 Cor 12:12). That he was remembered as a wonder-worker is clear, however, from the healings and other miracles attributed to him in the Acts of the Apostles (healings in Acts 14:10; 19:12; 20:10; 28:8f; other miracles in Acts 13:11; 14:3; 16:26; 19:11; 28:3-6). Paul nevertheless discounts the importance of miracles (1 Cor 1:22-25; 13:2), and, though he emphatically claims the charisma of speaking in tongues (1 Cor 14:20), he disparages it as having little value for building up the Church (1 Cor 13:1, etc.).

Any of the charismata (except apostleship itself) could be—and still can be—exercised more or less frequently by any member of the Christian community, but it seems that the necessities of community well-being resulted in the creation of certain offices of a more or less permanent nature. The only such offices mentioned by Paul himself are those of the bishops and deacons referred to in Phil 1:1. We do not know whether these officials were appointed by the apostle or elected by the community, nor do we really know their functions. From the basic meanings of the words (bishop, *episkopos* = overseer, and deacon, *diakonos* = servant or minister), however, it seems reasonable to suggest that these bishops and deacons exercised, on the one hand, the functions of guiding and presiding, and, on the other hand, the functions of service or ministry in general—including helping, sharing, and showing mercy.[65] Doubtless they were chosen in the first instance because they possessed the appropriate charismata (B7, D6, D2, B6, D5, D7); however, since the functions were necessary to the existence of the community, they soon came to be institutionalized.

These offices gained greatly in importance in the later

Church. Lists of qualifications for those who aspire to these offices are found in the Pastoral Epistles, and those for bishop (1 Tim 3:1-7; Tit 1:7-9) and deacon (1 Tim 3:8-13) are surprisingly similar. Among them we find a few echoes of the Pauline charismata: a bishop, for example, is required to be an apt teacher, as well as a manager (*proistamenos*) of his own household. The bishops and deacons came to exercise the ministry of the prophets and teachers and were honored accordingly (Didache 15:1f).

CHARISMATA OF POWER

The Greek word for "miracles" in the New Testament is *dynameis*, which in the singular (*dynamis*) means *power*. All the lists of charismata in 1 Corinthians include the ability to perform miracles (A5, B4, C4), and Paul says that he himself performed miracles in Corinth (2 Cor 12:12—RSV "mighty works"); however, we are not further enlightened as to the sort of miracles these were. Since Paul distinguished this gift from that of healing, he may have been using *dynameis* to denote what we sometimes call "nature miracles." This suggestion gains some support from Paul's reference to "moving mountains" (1 Cor 13:1f), where he makes the all-important connection with faith: faith is necessary to move mountains or to perform any other miracle.

The connection of miracles with faith is also prominent in the Synoptic Gospels, in which nearly two-thirds of the references to faith occur in relation to miracles, almost all of them in the sayings of Jesus—sayings that encourage faith (Mk 5:36; 9:23f; 11:22ff; Mt 9:28; Lk 17:6), commend faith (Mk 5:34; 10:52; Mt 8:10 = Lk 7:9; Mt 8:13; 15:28; Lk 7:50; 17:19), or rebuke lack of faith (Mk 4:40; 9:19; Mt 6:30; 14:31; 16:8; 17:20). The faith of those to whom Jesus ministered—not Jesus' own faith—was necessary complement to the exercise of God's power through him (cf. Mk 6:6 = Mt 13:58). "Faith in the recipient, as it were, completed the circuit so that the power could flow."[66]

Paul omits miracles (and healings) from his list of charismata in Rom 12:6-8, as he does that other "spectacular" gift, speaking with tongues. Even in 1 Corinthians he down-plays the importance of miracles (1 Cor 1:22-25, 13:2), though hardly as much as he disparages tongue-speaking. This may suggest that members of the Corinthian community especially esteemed this gift, as they did that of tongues; we do not know, however, whether any of them performed or pretended to perform miracles. There were unquestionably men and women in the Greco-Roman world—both within the Church and outside it—who were credited with the ability to work miracles,[67] and there are such people today. What is questionable is the efficacy of miracles for bringing people to Christian faith. Paul's Corinthian converts were not deterred from their erring ways by the recollection of the "signs, wonders, and mighty works" the apostle had wrought among them (2 Cor 12:12). It is perhaps most important when evaluating this gift to remember that Jesus himself refused to perform miracles for their own sake or for his own sake. Further, the grave danger exists of being led to worship the charisma or its possessor rather than the One who bestows it.

THE CHARISMA OF DISCERNMENT

The gift of discernment (1 Cor 12:10) provides a means for testing and evaluating all other charismata to determine whether they really have the Holy Spirit as their source. The importance of this charisma is obvious when we reflect that all the other gifts have been and still are capable of imitation. The New Testament itself mentions false apostles,[68] false prophets,[69] and false teachers,[70] and in our own time many leaders have arisen whose pseudo-charisma has enabled them to lead millions astray.[71] Miraculous healings were attributed in antiquity to the hero-god Asklepios,[72] the Neo-Pythagorean sage Apollonius of Tyana,[73] and the Roman Emperor Vespasian,[74] among many others, and similar healings have been ascribed in modern times to Anton Mesmer, the Russian monk Rasputin—a nickname meaning "dissolute"—, Phineas P. Quimby, and others outside or only marginally within the Christian fold.[75] Magicians and miracle-workers are met on many pages of ancient and medieval literature,[76] and in modern times "mediums" and "psychics" have claimed to possess miraculous powers.[77] Phenomena similar to glossolalia are far from rare outside the context of Christianity,[78] and, moreover, these phenomena may be unconsciously as well as deliberately imitated.[79] Finally, psychedelic drugs like LSD have been found to induce mental (and physical) states that are difficult to distinguish from those that occur in mystical ecstasy.[80]

Christians have the charisma of discernment because they have the Holy Spirit, the source of all true charismata:

> We have not received the spirit of the world, but the Spirit which is from God, that we might understand the things which have been bestowed on us by God. And we impart this in words not taught by human wisdom but taught by the Spirit, interpreting spiritual truths to those who possess the Spirit.
>
> (1 Cor 2:12f)

From 1 Cor 14:29 ("let the others weigh what is said"), it is clear that this charisma could be exercised by more than one person at the same time, i.e., by some or all of those hearing a (purportedly) inspired utterance: it was a shared conviction that the utterance was (or was not) in accord with the mind of God. This conviction might not be based on what we would regard as "rational" considerations (cf. 1 Cor 2:16—"But we have the mind of Christ" and 7:40—"I think that I have the Spirit of God"), but it might also be based on objective criteria that the charisma of discernment causes its recipients to perceive and recognize.

Among these criteria is the theological rule-of-thumb enunciated in 1 Cor 12:2—"No one speaking by the Spirit of God ever says 'Jesus is cursed!' and no one can say 'Jesus is Lord' except by the Holy Spirit," and in very similar terms in 1 Jn 4:2f—"By this you know the Spirit of God: every spirit which confesses that Jesus Christ has come in the flesh is of God, and every spirit which does not confess Jesus is not of God." Other criteria are moral and practical. The exercise of authentic gifts is accompanied by the fruit of the Spirit—"love, joy, peace, patience, kindness, goodness, faithfulness, gentleness, self-control"—and does not give rise to "enmity, strife, jealousy, selfishness, divisiveness, party spirit, [or] envy"

(Gal 5:19-22; cf. Mt 7:15; Eph 5:8-10). Authentic gifts build up the Church (1 Cor 14:4, 12, 26; cf. 12:7) and contribute to the growth and unity of the body of Christ. The charisma of discernment is not a spectacular gift, but one essential to uninterrupted progress in the building up of the Church.[81]

OTHER CHARISMATA

Nowhere does St. Paul suggest that his discussion of charismata is intended to be exhaustive. Indeed, the contrary is plainly implied by the differences between the Corinthian lists on the one hand and the Romans list on the other, as well as by Paul's mention of several charismata quite apart from the lists.[82] Nowhere, moreover, does St. Paul suggest that the outpouring of spiritual gifts was confined to the Church of his own time.

In the later books of the New Testament as well as in the writings of the sub-apostolic and later periods, to be sure, we do meet with concepts of charismata that differ more or less widely from those held by St. Paul. Both continuity and discontinuity can be seen in these later ideas, however, and there is no particular reason to regard the development as generally downward and deplorable.

Many early Church Fathers are in complete agreement with Paul on many points. They are unanimous in affirming the divine origin of charismata [83] as well as their diversity.[84] Many of the charismata mentioned by the Fathers are the same as or similar to those named in Paul's lists.[85] Much of what they say about the gifts also echoes the explicit or implicit opinions of Paul.[86]

The most frequently mentioned departure from the Pauline standard is probably the bestowal of the charisma of office by the laying on of hands:

> Do not neglect the gift (charisma) you have, which was given you by prophetic utterance when the elders laid their hands upon you.
>
> (1 Tim 4:14)

> I remind you to rekindle the gift that is within you through the
> laying on of my hands."
>
> (2 Tim 1:6)

However, even St. Paul could speak of "sharing" a charisma (Rom 1:11); if any charisma could be shared by its recipient, why not the charisma of office?[87]

A much greater departure from the earlier concept is to be seen in Origen's remark: "The charismata are given by God to those who have prepared themselves by faith and virtue to receive them."[88] This opinion is disputed, however, by Leontius of Jerusalem, who argues that the presence of charismata is not even proof of orthodoxy, much less piety.[89] St. Paul's own experience is surely conclusive evidence that "the Spirit blows where he wills." (Jn 3:8)

In more recent times grave differences of opinion have arisen about the continuing existence and availability of charismata in the Church—or outside of it, for that matter. On one side are the older Pentecostal groups and the Neo-Pentecostals in the mainline Churches, who vigorously affirm the activity of the Holy Spirit as manifested among them by spectacular charismata, especially glossolalia. On the other side, however, there is in the more traditional Churches a great reluctance to recognize the reality and value of charismatic phenomena; indeed, the members of these Churches tend to look on "enthusiasm" and "manifestations of the Spirit" with suspicion and even alarm.[90]

Both theological and practical reasons can be advanced for maintaining a cautious attitude toward the more extravagant claims of the Pentecostals and Neo-Pentecostals. From a theological point of view there is apprehension lest charismata purporting to involve new revelation content (i.e., prophecy) may seem to impugn the authority of Scripture. As Richard F. Lovelace wisely points out,

> It is extremely hazardous to give prophetic utterances and interpretations canonical authority. Any substantial dependence on these can easily lead to a neglect of the whole counsel of God already given to us and a failure in following the Holy Spirit's ordinary leading through the illumination of biblical knowledge.[91]

From a practical point of view there is the danger that Christians will come to believe false teaching and put their confidence in self-serving or misguided leaders. As we have seen, all the charismata can be imitated; and any charisma can, by misuse and abuse, lead to unedifying divisions and superstitions. Examples of such misuse and abuse can be found in every period of Christian history.[92]

The existence of counterfeit charismata does not disprove the existence of genuine charismata, however, and the fact that charismata may be abused and misused does not imply that no proper use for them exists. St. Paul's counsel is as valid today as it was when he first gave it to the Thessalonians: "Do not quench the Spirit, do not despise prophesying, but test everything: hold fast what is good." (1 Th 5:19-21).

The gifts of the Spirit are with us today, and they are with all of us. They are not limited to certain "elite" groups. To quote Lovelace once more,

> We should look forward to fully integrated churches in which all the gifts are practiced with . . . charity, . . . in place of churches which are homogeneously Pentecostal or non-Pentecostal, in which counterfeit gifts are being fostered in one area while genuine gifts are repressed in the other."[93]

Since we know that it is God's purpose to integrate and unite his Church (Jn 17:22f), we know that the true charismata of the Holy Spirit, received in faith and used in love, will not divide Christians but will bring them ever closer together. The Holy Spirit "blows where he wills." God may send the Spirit to those outside the Church to bring them in, as he did to St. Paul, but *we* must seek and find the Spirit *within* the Church. There we shall receive the Spirit and the Spirit's gifts and be made holy by the Spirit. To those outside we proclaim the message of reconciliation, which has been committed to us.

4

The Gifts of God in the New Creation

Part Two: The Church of the Present and Future

The Christian Gospel is good news. It proclaims the forgiving act of God in Jesus Christ, which has set straight our relation to God. In traditional theology this act is often called the Atonement, which means quite literally "at-one-ment," the making whole of the shattered bond uniting us to God. As a consequence of that reconciliation we discover that all other broken relationships—with ourselves, with other people, with the world—are, potentially at least, restored. They are full of new possibilities. Lives are renewed by the gift of the Spirit of Christ. Baptism invites us into community where this gift is available. The Eucharist draws us into communion again and again with the one who gave himself for the life of the world.

And, as he gave himself for us and gives himself to us, we in turn give ourselves to him. We put ourselves at his disposal, for the renewing of the lives of the people of God. We give ourselves ritually and liturgicallly at the Eucharist in an act of commitment or recommitment. "Here we offer and present unto thee, O Lord, ourselves..." (*BCP*, p. 336). What is more, we seek to translate that commitment into action beyond the eucharistic service, by using the gifts bestowed on us to love and serve our neighbors. In so doing we pray that God's new creation will be further realized.

In this chapter we shall explore some of these aspects of the new creation: God's reconciling of the world in Christ; Baptism as entrance into the new creation; Eucharist as participation in the new creation; all these as the gift of God the Spirit.

GOD'S HEALING ACT: RECONCILIATION AS GIFT

The new creation and everything connected with it is gift. "Behold, I make all things new," God announces near the end of the last book of the Bible, the Revelation to John. These words are spoken at the climax of a strangely powerful and majestic series of visions that portray the triumph of Christ over the powers of evil. It is worth noting that this climax is not the end of the world, but rather its new beginning. To be exact, this book speaks of the end of the world as it is, fractured by human rebelling; but its final picture is of a new world, the world as God wills it to be. There is harmony all around because there is peace between God and the creation:

> I saw the holy city, new Jerusalem, coming down out of heaven from God, prepared as a bride adorned for her husband; and I heard a great voice from the throne saying, "Behold, the dwelling of God is with his people. He will dwell with them, and they shall be his people, and God himself shall be with them; he will wipe away every tear from their eyes, and death shall be no more, neither shall there be mourning, nor crying, nor pain any more, for the former things have passed away.
>
> (Rev 21:2-4)

It is worth pointing out that this new world is not a reproduction of the Garden of Eden. The citizens of this heavenly city are not innocents, like Adam and Eve. They have lived through the dangers and temptations of life. They have experienced grief, pain, and death. The Bible, in other words, does not envision the return of humanity to its starting point. That vision would make human history meaningless. All that has been experienced as a result of our exercise of freedom, with all its attendant cost, would be wiped out. The whole human story of struggle, pain, failure, achievement, success, would—in this long run—be meaningless, "a tale told by an idiot, signifying nothing," in Macbeth's desperate phrase (V, 5; 1126-28).

In biblical perspective, the human story reaches a conclusion different from its starting point, different and better. It is better because human beings have used their first gift of freedom "to make something of themselves." They have entered the world of sin and death. But, in an extraordinary way, God has dealt with those effects of the exercise of our freedom by means of a new gift: the gift of his Son. By this action creation has been renewed. And the renewal is not only future hope. It begins now, in the present time. God gives us his Spirit now, as a guarantee and foretaste of the complete renewal of all things. "Therefore," wrote St. Paul,

> if anyone is in Christ, he is a new creation; the old has passed away; behold, the new has come. All this is from God, who through Christ reconciled us to himself and gave us the ministry of reconciliation.
>
> (2 Cor 5:17-18)

God's act of reconciliation was understood by the first Christians to be identical to the life, death, and new life of Jesus of Nazareth. Through Jesus all our relationships have been restored and redeemed.

Jesus enjoyed an unbroken relationship with God. Such is the picture the New Testament draws of him. "No one knows the Son except the Father, and no one knows the Father except the Son and anyone to whom the Son chooses to reveal him" (Mt 11:27). "I and the Father are one" (Jn 10:30). He "in every respect has been tempted as we are, yet without sin" (Heb 4:15). Jesus' life was a whole life, the gift of God through the Spirit from the very beginning and throughout.

It would be interesting to write an account of Jesus' life as the work of the Spirit, using New Testament records.[1] The New Testament community saw Jesus as conceived by the Spirit

(Lk 1:34f), baptized by the Spirit (Mk 1:1-11), driven by the Spirit into the wilderness to be tempted (Mk 1:12)—one might infer that he resisted his temptations by the power of the Spirit. He preached, healed, and taught in the power of the Spirit (Lk 4:14).

Jesus' death was understood to have restored the broken relationships of his disciples. Through it they entered into his wholeness. Since the sacrificial system was supposed to restore communion with God, Jesus' death was identified as a sacrifice, because it did restore communion with God. The interpretation of Jesus' crucifixion as a sacrifice is, to be sure, by no means an obvious one. Hundreds and thousands of victims were crucified by the Romans, including the two thieves or brigands who hung on either side of Jesus on Calvary. Their deaths are not counted as sacrifices, at least in the technical sense of the term.

But from a very early date Christians took Jesus' death as sacrificial. St. Paul spoke of "Christ, our paschal lamb, sacrificed for us" (1 Cor 5:7). The Epistle to the Hebrews describes the death and exaltation of Jesus as the fulfillment of the whole round of sacrifices carried on in the Jewish temple.

> For Christ has entered, not into a sanctuary made with hands, a copy of the true one, but into heaven itself, now to appear in the presence of God on our behalf. Nor was it to offer himself repeatedly, as the high priest [on Atonement Day, cf. Lev 16] enters the Holy Place yearly with blood not his own; for then he would have had to suffer repeatedly since the foundation of the world. But as it is, he has appeared once for all at the end of the age to put away sin by the sacrifice of himself.
>
> (Heb 9:24-26)

Why the sacrificial language? James Muilenburg says that the Hebrew people, like everyone in the ancient world, crossed from the realm of the profane into the realm of the sacred by sacrificial gifts.[2] Sacrifice established communion with God. The joyful, virtually incredible discovery of the first Christian disciples was that after the death of Jesus, communion with God had been restored. What the ancient sacrifices had done at best imperfectly was now, they saw, accomplished. The death of Jesus was not a proper sacrifice according to temple rules and regulations. The place was wrong, the officiants were wrong, the victim was wrong. Yet the results were those for which people had been hoping and longing: "God and sinners reconciled." By experience, Jesus' death was a sacrifice.

The chief evidence that the reconciliation had occurred was the resurrection of Jesus from the dead. Those who gathered to break bread in the Upper Room, in the Inn along the road to Emmaus, on the shore of the Sea of Galilee, knew Jesus to be alive. Death, that ultimate symbol of broken relationships, had been overcome.

What was more, the disciples' relation to Jesus was restored. They had deserted and denied him. His death had severed a relationship already twisted by their disloyalty. The reality of Christ's living presence after Easter is nowhere better shown than by the fact that Peter and the others knew themselves to be forgiven. As the Dutch theologian Edward Schillebeeckx has put it, "a dead man does not proffer forgiveness."[13] By the power of God shown in the resurrection of Christ, the power of death was overthrown and the effects of sin overcome. What a gift! St. Paul suggests that it, too, is a gift of the Spirit. For Jesus was, he writes, "descended from David according to the flesh and designated Son of God in power according to the Spirit of holiness by his resurrection from the dead" (Rom 1:4).

We must admit that, so far, sin and death have been defeated only in this one instance. But that experience was so powerful that the disciples quickly grasped its significance for all human life. The kingdom of God that Jesus and John the Baptist had proclaimed had arrived. A whole new creation had begun "in power and beginning."[4] It had not been established in its fullness, that was clear. Evidence of sin and death was (and is) pervasive. But a radical new possibility had been introduced into human history: the transforming power of God's love as seen in the life of Jesus. Like a patient who received the injection of a powerful drug that will cure his disease and yet still suffers from it, the old creation has received a new gift: the introduction of the reconciling, forgiving, love of God. Although the effects of the disease persist and may, in fact, get worse before they disappear, the outcome is sure. This gift of love of God might also be identified as a gift of the Spirit, of the Spirit of Christ, which is love.[5]

Notice how the effects of reconciliation spread: The relation between Jesus and the disciples is restored. The disciples renew their relation to one another. A community is formed of which it can be said that one passes from death to life because one loves one's brothers and sisters in Christ (1 Jn 3:14). In Christ the community becomes a family, and because of the love of that family one passes from death to life, in the Spirit of Jesus.

An even larger realm of reconciliation appears. Not only these, but all relationships are being made new "in power and beginning." At the first Christian Pentecost the eleven in Jerusalem received the gift of the Spirit and "spoke in other tongues as the Spirit gave them utterance" (Acts 2:4). Citizens from countries all over the then known world heard them speaking their own language (Acts 2:6). The confusion of tongues in which the Tower of Babel story ended is reversed. Most New Testament scholars agree that the undoing of the alienation represented by the Tower of Babel story in Genesis is at least one meaning of speaking in tongues in the Pentecost story. The hostility of the nations is healed "in power and beginning" by the gift of the Spirit.

What is more, St. Paul turns attention to inner life and the broken relation of self to self. That, too, has been set straight "in principle."

> For I delight in the law of God in my inmost self, but I see in my members another law at war with the law of my mind and making me captive to the law of sin which dwells in my members. Wretched man that I am! Who will deliver me from this body of death? Thanks be to God through Jesus Christ our Lord!
> (Rom 7:22-25)

This inner reconciliation, this re-creation of the "inmost self," is also a gift of the Spirit, as the eighth chapter of Romans makes unmistakably clear. "For the law of the Spirit of life in Christ Jesus has set me free from the law of sin and death" (Rom 8:2). The whole chapter elaborates this theme. Luther once called the Epistle to the Romans "the clearest gospel of them all."[6]

So the features of the new creation begin to emerge from various quarters, in various stages of development and understanding. It is by no means a systematic or uniform picture. Some people expected that the work of new creation which was beginning in so many different ways would be completed in a short time. Today we know that the time will be long. Without some direct knowledge of the Spirit, we might convince ourselves that the whole New Testament hope for a new creation was nothing but wishful thinking, a pipe dream. But the experience of renewal in the Church today is evidence on the other side. The gifts of the Spirit continue to be given in our time, and the triumphs of God's love continue to amaze us.

In the second chapter we associated the gifts of God with human freedom, in the sense of the freedom of the self from the self, the achievement of self-awareness, and therefore the emergence of true selves. In the new creation we have the gift of freedom in a new sense: freedom from fear of death and from the effects of sin, accomplished by the reconciling love of Christ. This gift of the Spirit is thus a gift of renewed and redeemed freedom (cf. 2 Cor 3:17; Gal 5:1). As a result of this new freedom we are free in a new dimension: free to love, to love God, to love one another, to love ourselves, to love the world God made. We are free to give ourselves with new depth and courage. We are free at last—in power and beginning.

All this—the life of Jesus our Lord, his sacrificial death and resurrection, his forgiveness of our sins, his reconciliation of the world and of the anxious selves in it—all this is the gift of God the Spirit. How does it come to us? How can we know it and appropriate it?

ENTRANCE INTO THE NEW CREATION: BAPTISM AS GIFT

Word and Sacraments as Means of Grace

"Means of grace" is a familiar Prayer Book phrase (*BCP*, p. 58; cf. pp. 857,872). It refers to ways in which God's gifts are understood to be communicated in the life of the church. The means of grace are customarily identified as Word, by which is meant the Bible and preaching, and (perhaps more usually) Sacraments. Two thousand years after the reconciling event of Jesus Christ, men and women continue to experience the same reconciliation and to receive the same gifts of the Spirit that were bestowed on the first Christian communities. They are distributed to us by the proclamation of the Word and the administration of the Sacraments. We enter the new creation through Baptism; we continually participate in its life through the Eucharist.[7]

In the next two sections of this chapter we shall explore the "means of grace."[8] Before we begin, however, we should remind ourselves of the observation of the thirteenth-century theologian Peter Lombard, who wrote, "God is not tied to the Sacraments, but we are."[9] It would be misleading and in fact untrue if we were to give the impression that God gives his many and various gifts only through the Church's official channels. Too many people who have nothing to do with the Church have been blessed in too many ways to make such an exclusive statement tenable in any way. On the other hand, when we approach the subject not from the perspective of God's freedom to grant gifts at pleasure but from the perspective of our own need and search for them, we can recognize that Word and Sacraments are means readily accessible to us, that God has promised to be with us through them, and that we would be strangely perverse to neglect them and look for others.

The Background of Christian Baptism

There is something wonderfully specific about the Sacraments. Why water? What does that have to do with the reconciling love of God? There is a similar, irreducible surprise in bread and wine. What do they have to do with the new creation? We shall consider Baptism first.

First of all, we notice that the Church has accepted the rite of Baptism in water in the name of the Lord Jesus, or in the name of the Trinity, as commanded and instituted by the risen Lord himself:

> Go therefore and make disciples of all nations, baptizing them in
> the name of the Father and of the Son and of the Holy Spirit,
> teaching them to observe all that I have commanded you, and lo,
> I am with you always, to the close of the age.
>
> (Mt 28:19f)

Baptism in water has been the virtually universal rite of initiation into the Christian Church ever since (the Society of
Friends being an exception). Why Baptism? Because Jesus
commanded it.

There is more to it than bare obedience. We know that Jesus
did not invent Baptism. Baptism was, and still is, the way
Gentiles who have been converted to the Jewish faith enter the
ranks of Israel. John the Baptist urged his contemporaries,
who were already Jews, to be baptized. Jesus was baptized by
John. John's baptism brings to light a whole new dimension of
meaning in the rite.

John connected Baptism with the near approach of God's
Kingdom. There was an expectation entertained by some of the
later Old Testament prophets that when God acted to establish
the Kingdom, God would first gather the people from all the
places where they were living outside the land of Israel. There
would be a new Exodus, a new march through the wilderness,
a new crossing of the Jordan river. The Second Isaiah described
this version of the future unforgettably (chs. 40-55. esp.
43:16-21), as did Ezekiel (ch. 36), Zephaniah (ch. 3, esp. v. 20),
and Zechariah (ch. 8, esp. v. 7). In Ezekiel's version, this final
gathering of the people of God would be accompanied by a
kind of baptism. He wrote:

> I will take you from the nations and gather you from all countries,
> and bring you into your own land. I will sprinkle clean water
> upon you, and you shall be clean from all your unclean-
> nesses. . . . A new heart will I give you and a new spirit I will put
> within you.
>
> (Ezek 36:24-26)

John the Baptist inherited this expectation, as did all Isra-
elites. But he took it seriously, as we know the residents of
Qumran—who produced the Dead Sea Scrolls—did also. He

believed this event to be so close that he urged everyone he could to go down to the Jordan and be baptized on the spot, so that they would belong to the kingdom when it was established. "Repent and be baptized!" was John's message before it was taken over by the Christian Church. When Peter told his hearers on Pentecost to repent and be baptized in the name of Jesus Christ, he held out implicitly the same hope that John held—that God was about to establish his rule. Baptism came into the practice of the Church already freighted with ideas of deliverance, renewal, and cleansing by the power of God.

Baptism on Pentecost and Beyond

We can learn more about Baptism as a means of cummunicating the reconciling love of God if, with this background in mind, we look closely at the events on the first Christian Pentecost, which culminated in the Baptism of a large crowd— "three thousand souls," we are told (Acts 2:41).

Preaching

It began with the sermon Peter preached in the power of the Holy Spirit. The sermon itself was the gift of the Spirit, and through it the Spirit was given to its hearers. One of the reasons sermons are often unpopular is that so many are not the gift of the Spirit and are not inspiring. The fact is, however, that people are moved to seek the gifts of God in Christ by hearing what those gifts are. Apart from a declaration of that good news, it is difficult to see what would have moved people to seek Baptism on that Pentecost.

If one were to study the accounts of Baptism in Acts, one would learn that in almost every instance Baptism was preceded by some form of telling the story of Jesus, usually as the climax of a recital of all God's works of deliverance. That is true on Pentecost (Acts 2), in the case of the Ethiopian eunuch (Acts 8:26-40), in the case of Paul—if we remember that he had witnessed Stephen's martyrdom and knew enough about Christians to think them worth persecuting! It was true for Cornelius the centurion, whom Peter baptized after having been really converted again himself, to take up a ministry to the Gentiles (Acts 10:1-48, esp. vv. 34-43).

There are apparent exceptions to this rule. As far as the record goes, Paul baptized his jailer in Philippi without benefit of sermon (Acts 16:25-34), and the sermon at Ephesus before Paul baptized some disciples there was apparently minimal (Acts 9:1-6). But sooner or later the meaning of what Christ has done for us has to be stated or communicated in some way. If Baptism loses its connection with the cross and resurrection, it loses its Christian meaning. Something must happen to stir the heart. One is moved by someone else or by something else to ask, "What shall I do?"

The answer, then as now, is deceptively simple: "Repent and be baptized in the name of Jesus Christ, and you shall receive the gift of the Holy Spirit" (Acts 2:38).

Repentance

Repentance comes first.[10] One of the Greek words used for "repent" in the New Testament (*epistrephein*) means literally "to turn" or "to turn around." "Turn from your former ways!" was the constant plea of Israel's prophets when Israel became faithless. But the call to repentance is more than a demand to stop doing evil things and to shape up, as another important word for "repent" indicates. This is *metanoein*, which means "to change one's mind." To what shall one's mind be changed? St. Paul makes this perfectly clear: "Have this mind among yourselves which is yours in Christ Jesus" (Phil 2:5), and again, "Do not be conformed to this world, but be transformed by the renewal of your minds" (Rom 12:2). The New English Bible makes these familiar verses even clearer: "Let your bearing toward one another arise out of your life in Christ Jesus," and "Let your minds be remade and your whole nature thus transformed." If that were to happen, we would have no desire to do evil things.

Humanly speaking, of course, it is impossible to repent in this full sense. It would be lifting one's self by one's bootstraps. But help comes from outside to make repentance possible. How can that be so? We should realize that when the necessity of repentance and the transformation and renewal of minds is laid on hearers in the Biblical tradition—Old Testament or New—it is done in the context of preaching or of some pro- clamation of the Word that has been inspired by the Spirit. The very fact that hearers ask, "What shall we do?" is evidence that the Spirit has already been introduced into their hearts and has begun to work.

Thus the summons to repent, to "let your minds be made new and your whole nature thus transformed," is not addressed to an unbeliever's impotent will, but to a person in whom the love of God has already begun to move. Repentance is itself first a gift, before it is our act. Turn! Let the Spirit finish in you what the Spirit has already begun through the proclamation of the Word.

Baptism

Water in Christian Baptism has rich and complex meanings. Some of them have carried over from the Jewish forms of the rite, as we have seen. The prayer of Thanksgiving over the water in the Prayer Book holds them up to view (*BCP*, p. 306). "Over it the Holy Spirit moved at the beginning of creation." We recall that all forms of life on our planet are said to have emerged from water. "Through it you led the children of Israel out of their bondage in Egypt into the land of promise." We recall the whole Old Testament drama of human disobedience and God's rescue that prepared the way for Christ. "In it your son Jesus received the baptism of John and was anointed by the Holy Spirit as the Messiah . . . ." We have already called attention to this part of the story.

The prayer continues: "In it we are buried with Christ in his death. By it we share in his resurrection. Through it we are reborn by the Holy Spirit." The language echoes a New Testament passage about Baptism:

> Do you not know that all of us who have been baptized into Christ Jesus were baptized into his death? We were buried therefore with him by baptism into death, so that as Christ was raised from the dead by the glory of the Father, we too might walk in newness of life.
>
> (Rom 6:3f)

On Pentecost Peter told the crowd to be baptized "in the name of Jesus Christ." We can see that Baptism "in the name of Jesus Christ" is a dramatic re-enactment of the dying and rising of Christ. Earlier forms of baptism may have been designed as re-enactments of the crossing of the Red Sea or of the crossing of the Jordan as a prelude to the establishment of the Kingdom of God. But for Christians it means dying with Christ so that they can live with Christ in a life renewed by the Spirit. What is accomplished in Baptism for an individual is no different from what was accomplished by the death and resurrection of Christ for the world. Baptism is a means of entering the new creation that God effected in him.

How? How do the gifts of the Spirit, which were lavished on the world in Christ, flow to us through the Sacrament of Baptism? It is difficult—perhaps impossible—to make the answer to that question speak to the heart of a reader of this book. But the form of the answer is easy to write. The Holy Spirit enlivens the sacraments. The Holy Spirit uses the sacramental action to transmit the reality of Christ that underlies the sacrament. The Spirit makes the gifts from God available to each one of us. In the Prayer Book service, the water is "sanctified by the power of the Holy Spirit" (*BCP*, p. 307); and we give thanks that "by water and the Holy Spirit you have bestowed upon these your servants the forgiveness of sins and raised them to the new life of grace" (*BCP*, p. 308). It is the way of the Spirit to use ordinary things to distribute God's extraordinary gifts, as it was the way of the Spirit to embody God's very life in the life of a human being to bring about the new creation. It is the experience of the Church that it has happened so and that it continues to happen so. How it happens is an abiding mystery.

In Power and Beginning

God's work in Christ transforms the world "in power and beginning." Christ's work in us, in Baptism, transforms us "in power and beginning." Baptism is the beginning of our life in the Spirit. The process will be complete only in the Kingdom of God. Baptism does not complete the new creation for an individual man or woman, any more than the event of Christ completed the new creation of the world. Christians still kill, commit adultery, steal, and lie; oppression, lust, and crime still stalk the world, and Christians still engage in them to our endless shame.

Yet something is complete at Baptism, just as something is complete in the death and resurrection of Jesus Christ. The vision of the rule of God is complete. With eyes opened to the reality of God in Christ, one can see the kingdom of justice and peace as clearly and palpably as one can see a finished flower in a germinating seed. More than that, no new and different power is needed to complete the process. What Christ has done is sufficient. The love he embodied and introduced into the world—and, by our baptism, into our lives—the love that "is patient and kind, not jealous or boastful, not arrogant or rude, . . . [that] bears all things, believes all things, hopes all things, endures all things" (1 Cor 13:4-7), this love will complete the transformation it has begun.

Meanwhile the Spirit has been given us as a guarantee, as the New Testament says over and over again (cf. 2 Cor 1:22; Eph 4:30), and we "groan inwardly" (Rom 8:23) until the new creation is finished.

The Way of the Spirit

How does love bring about the transformation of individuals? Love's ways are various, surprising, and as enigmatic as the world itself. In general one observes two things, one connected with our sin and the healing of distorted relations and the other connected with our finiteness and the acceptance of our limitation.

With respect to sin and distorted relationships, love means forgiveness. Baptism is for the forgiveness of sins. The example of Jesus Christ is an example of forgiveness, and the power of the Spirit that comes from him moves us toward forgiveness. Just as the forgiving love of Christ set the original disciples into a right relation with God and the rest of their relationships were consequently transformed, so through Baptism Christians have access to the grace of forgiving love, through the Spirit.[11]

We learn to forgive one another. We become members of a forgiving community—in power and beginning—and in that context of love, we enter into a new and improved relationship with ourselves. We discover a new freedom, that freedom from sin and death of which we have already spoken. We accept ourselves as God accepts us, "just as I am, without one plea." It is a new gift of ourselves from God, the gift of the Spirit in redemption and reconciliation.

As part of that gift we learn to accept our limitations, too. In the new creation, especially at its beginning (which we enter at Baptism), we are still finite, weak, limited creatures. We do not have all gifts. We cannot do everything. But—in spite of all that—we discover "the courage to be,"[12] the courage to be who we are in the face of life's sometimes cruel limitations. We acknowledge and celebrate the gifts God has given us in the first creation, our inherent talents and aptitudes we discussed in chapter two. These will be no different from what they were before, but we regard them with new understanding and new satisfaction. Moreover, if God chooses to bestow on us one or more of the special gifts of the Holy Spirit, the charismata the New Testament promises and experience teaches us to expect, we shall acknowledge and celebrate these also, gratefully using them, like all our other gifts, not for any selfish purpose but for the building up of the Church.

Two Questions about Baptism

Before we leave the discussion of Baptism, however, we must consider two problems that often have exercised the Christian Church in the past and have recently come to the fore again. The first is the effectiveness of water Baptism. The second is the propriety of infant Baptism.

The Effectiveness of Water Baptism

The experience of the Spirit, which some people have in renewal movements, is sometimes so rich and impressive that it seems to them that they have never known the Spirit at all before. This new experience comes to them as their real introduction to the Christian faith. They identify it with the "baptism of the Holy Spirit" that John the Baptist expected the Messiah to bring (Mk 1:8) and that the risen Christ himself promised (Acts 1:5). Their prior water Baptism then seems to them insignificant. They set it aside as a means of initiation into the Church and into the Spirit. This teaching and the attitude behind it cause considerable confusion.

As we have seen, the normal way the Spirit of Christ has been accessible to individuals in the Church has been, from the very beginning, through repentance, water Baptism, and consequent incorporation into the Church, the body of Christ. We have recognized that repentance implies the Spirit has already been active in a preliminary way through some form of proclamation of the Word, before an individual responds by seeking Baptism. Nevertheless, the promise of God, as the Church has received it, is connected with water baptism. Membership in the Church is connected with water baptism. Without wishing to "tie God the Sacraments," we must conclude, as the Prayer Book catechism does, that one becomes a Christian when one is baptized in water and the Holy Spirit.

This statement, of course, does not end the matter. It is certainly true that one grows in the life of the Spirit. The influence of the Spirit is more obvious in some than in others, and some people are more aware of the Spirit than are others. Some people may not be at all self-conscious of their relationship to God through the Spirit, but neighbors and acquaintances may see Spirit active through and through in the words and deeds of those who are not themselves aware. The Christian community has ample room for all sorts and conditions of men and women, and for those also who suddenly have new access to spiritual insight.

There is much to be experienced in the life of the Spirit beyond Baptism. It is always appropriate to desire and pray for a deeper relationship to the Spirit, and it is always reasonable to expect times when that relationship will be more vivid than at others. Nevertheless the whole thrust of the Bible, church tradition, and the experience of living Christians who are wise in the Spirit's ways is to insist that the Spirit is normally made available to us at the outset by repentance and Baptism in water—our initiation into the community of the Holy Spirit. It is only confusing, and in the end disruptive, to speak of two Baptisms, one in water and another in the Holy Spirit, and then to imply that only the second counts. In New Testament perspective, Christian Baptism is Baptism in the Holy Spirit.[13]

Infant Baptism
What about infant Baptism, then? Infants cannot respond to preaching in any obvious sense. They are not apparently able to repent. Should they be baptized? What is their relation to the Spirit of God?

The history of infant Baptism is obscure. There is no certain evidence in the New Testament either to confirm or deny it. It is suggestive that, when Paul baptized the jailer in Philippi, his whole family was included, and even more suggestive when one notices that, in the Jewish practice of Baptism, whole families—young and old alike—were baptized together. For Baptism was a way of joining Israel, of entering the covenant with Israel's God. Even the youngest members of families were, and are, granted that status. It seems at least reasonable to suppose that, from the beginning of the Church, whole families—young and old together—were included in the New Covenant as they were in the Old. The baptismal rite of Hippolytus of Rome, early in the third century, makes explicit provision for infants.

It is true that for several centuries the custom was to postpone Baptism for as long as possible, for many in the early Church believed that mortal sins committed after Baptism could not be forgiven. But as soon as the question of full availability of pardon and grace—even for post-baptismal sins—was clarified, infant Baptism became prevalent. By the seventh or eighth century, liturgical texts assumed that candidates were infants; by the thirteenth or fourteenth century, Baptism within eight days of birth was required.

What shall we say about the practice today? Infants cannot respond to the preaching of the Gospel. Yet it is clear that infants can and do respond to the love of parents communicated with more than words in all those subtle words love knows how to find. Through the love of Christian parents, which "bears all things, believes all things, hopes all things, endures all things" (1 Cor 13:7) the Spirit can be communicated at noncognitive levels. It can begin to refashion and reshape the whole being of a person long before the person is aware of it. The very formative process of a Christian family bears witness to the reality of such love. If repentance is, as we suggested earlier, a matter of "letting yor minds be remade and your whole nature thus transformed," there seems to be nothing to prevent this process from occurring in the youngest child. And if Baptism is Baptism for the forgiveness of sins, how quickly children can forgive us!

There is also the question of membership. It is surely as important for Christian families today as it has been in Jewish families to understand that the whole family is together in its covenant relation with God.

In consideration of the promises of God, the unity and integrity of the family, and the understanding of the operation of the Spirit of love at sub-cognitive levels—in children and adults alike! there seems to be nothing to preclude, and a great deal to encourage, the continued practice of infant Baptism. Infants also belong to the new creation, in power and beginning.

CONTINUING PARTICIPATION IN THE NEW CREATION: EUCHARIST AS GIFT

We become members of the Church and enter the new creation through Christian Baptism. Thomas Aquinas was of the opinion that if a person never sinned after Baptism, never did anything to fall away from the grace of God, Baptism would be the only necessary sacrament.[14] We all surely recognize, however, as St. Thomas did, that we do fall away from the grace of God, and that we do need other means of grace to enable us to continue our life in the Spirit. Chief among them is the Eucharist.

Background of the Christian Eucharist

Many of the things we said about Baptism do not need to be repeated. In its own particular and specific way, the Eucharist is a gift of the healing love of Christ, just as is Baptism.[15] It is effective among us in much the same ways, indescribable as they are, as Baptism. It, too is God's gift to us in power and beginning. But we need to look more closely at the specific elements of the Eucharist. Why bread and wine? What do they have to do with the reconciling love of God? Why should they be given to us as means of grace?

The Church has received the Eucharist as commanded and instituted by Jesus himself. The scene at the Last Supper when Jesus said, "Do this in remembrance of me," is too vivid to need rehearsal. Has any other command in history been so amply obeyed, at all times and in all places, under all circumstances?

But, as in the case of Baptism, there is more to it than bare obedience. Eucharist is a particularly rich symbolic action. In many ways it is the "means of grace" par excellence. Eating together is a primordial expression of human community. Feeding is a deep symbol of love and participation. It is an obvious and profound sign of the sharing of what one has and of what gives life. For Christians it has become the most frequently sought, most highly prized means of access to Christ. He gave himself for us once. He gives himself continually to us in the Eucharist.

But there is still more. The Eucharist, like Baptism, is freighted with Jewish ideas and hopes and dreams, of deliverance, renewal, forgiveness, and communion through the power of God.

It is not necessary for our purposes to investigate the large amount of material that has been written about the background of the Eucharist.[16] We must observe, however, that, like Baptism, the Church did not invent it. It has its roots in Jewish rituals, reinterpreted in the light of the new creation.

One of the historical problems a close reading of the New Testament brings to light is whether or not the Last Supper was a Passover meal. If if was, then all the overtones of God's deliverance of his people from Egypt and their hope for the establishment of God's rule in the near future—"Next year in Jerusalem!" is the prayer at each Jewish Passover Seder—would have been expressed there. Those accents are parallel to those we discovered about Baptism. What is more, the Passover Seder provides a suggestive parallel for the identification of the elements: "This is my body . . . ; this cup is the new covenant in my blood" (1 Cor 11:24-25; cf. Lk 22:19f). The host at the Seder says—of the bread, "This is the bread of affliction which your fathers did eat when they came out of Egypt."

On the other hand, if the Last Supper was not a Passover meal, as the chronology of St. John's Gospel suggests, then this meal was the last in a series of fellowship meals (*chabûrôth*) Jesus ate with his disciples. At it he looked forward to the great Messianic feast in the Kingdom of God: "I shall not drink again of the fruit of the vine until that day when I drink it new with you in my Father's Kingdom" (Mk 14:25). This interpretation of the Last Supper makes it easier to understand why the earliest Christians broke bread daily (Acts 2:46) rather than yearly, as we would expect if the Passover were the model.[17]

Fortunately, it is not necessary to choose between these two interpretations. For it is certain that the Last Supper occurred at Passover time. Passover was in the air. The meal was colored both by Passover expectations and by the particular hopes of Jesus' disciples. The Eucharist, we might say, is grafted onto existing Jewish liturgical models—Passover and fellowship meals, occasions at which people ate together to celebrate events in history through which God had delivered his people from their enemies and to express a commonly shared hope in the fulfillment of those purposes.

He Was Made Known to Them in the Breaking of Bread

The Christian Eucharist adds to this already rich symbolic action an utterly transforming element: the crucial and obtrusive identification of the bread and wine. "This is my body . . . this is my blood . . . " (Mk 14:22, 24; Mt 26:26, 28). The Eucharist becomes a vehicle for sharing the life of Jesus, a vehicle for entering into communion with God, a "means of grace." We "do this in remembrance of" Jesus. We remember his death, resurrection, and ascension. We remember these acts and events in the presence of God; and, because all times and places are equally present to God, Jesus' death and new life in particular are present in our own time and place. They are not present because we remember them: they are present because we are caught up in this action. As in Baptism we die with Christ and are raised to a new life with him, by the power of the Spirit, so in the Eucharist we appropriate his sacrificial death and his new life for ourselves by eating bread and drinking wine—by the power of the Spirit. What Jesus did for the whole creation once for all he makes over to us individually, through the Spirit, in this sacramental act.

Eucharist is participation in forgiveness. "The Blood of the new Covenant . . . is shed for you and for many for the forgiveness of sins" (*BCP*, p. 363; cf. Mt 26:28). It is participation in eternal life, "the holy food and drink of our new and unending life in him" (*BCP*, ibid.; cf. 1 Cor 10:16). It is participation in the new creation (*BCP*, ibid.).

Eucharist Is the Gift of the Spirit

The Eucharist is not only a gift of the Spirit ("subjective"), a charisma from God, as some church Fathers held,[18] it is the gift of the Spirit ("objective"), that is, the Spirit is given in it and through it. The Spirit both vivifies the enacted drama of death and resurrection and opens our eyes to perceive Christ present. "Sanctify [this bread and wine] by your Holy Spirit to be for your people the Body and Blood of your Son . . . . Sanctify us also, that we may faithfully receive this sacrament" (*BCP*, ibid.). This is not a new gift. The Spirit makes available to us the reconciling love of Christ, by which all the relations of sinful men and women are healed and the world made new, in power and beginning.

Eucharist As Our Self-Offering and the Offering of Our Gifts for the Sake of the World

> Thou didst give thyself for me,
> Now I give myself to thee,
>
> (Hymnal 1940, #190)

We must examine more closely one element of eucharistic action, that of self-offering. It is mentioned explicitly in two places: at the offering before the eucharistic prayer and in the final act of the service.

The first self-offering is represented by "bread and wine, and money or other gifts" (*BCP*, p. 361). They are presented and placed on the altar at the time of the offertory. Money is the product and sign of our labor. It stands for us. It is well known that our pocket-book nerve is the most sensitive of all. The connection between our money and our selves is very close. It is a good symbol for us, just as we are—a strange combination of wisdom, skill, and folly, of altruism and greed, of love and sin, all together.

Some of the money we give to the Church goes to buy bread and wine. Bread and wine, in turn, are the result and symbol of the labor of others: those who grow grain, transport it, manufacture flour and bake bread, and those who grow grape vines and manufacture wine. If we were to trace out the whole list of people who had some part in the placing of bread on a dinner table or on our altar, it would include representatives of most of our society: agriculture, transportation, commerce, manufacture of machines, governmental services, and doubtless many more. All of that is also offered in the course of eucharistic action.

Baptism and Eucharist differ in this dimension of self-offering. Baptism is our initiation into the new creation. We might say, in fact, that Baptism is the offering of ourselves to God. We ourselves become the symbol of the death and resurrection of Christ through the baptismal action. We are buried with Christ in his death and raised to a new life in his love.

The Eucharist involves different symbols. Men and women already baptized come to the Eucharist for renewal of the gift of grace. We have already offered ourselves in response to God's reconciling love. We have already received the gift of the Spirit. Now we want to renew that relationship and continue in that love. So we offer ourselves again—symbolically this time. We offer what we can offer, imperfect, incomplete, flawed though that may be. If we did not do that, if we withheld ourselves and did not present to God what we have made of ourselves, under these symbols of money, bread, and wine, to receive the renewed gifts of grace, it is doubtful that we seriously desired to continue in the new creation.

There is a second self-offering, a final giving of ourselves at this service. It is at least as significant at the first and in a certain sense authenticates the whole action. At the end of the service the whole congregation offers itself to love and serve God in the world, and every member joins in the prayer for grace "to do all such good works as thou hast prepared for us to walk in" (*BCP*, p. 339) or "to love and serve you with gladness and singleness of heart" (*BCP*, p. 365).

The Eucharist is a gift of God. It is the gift of a new freedom to be ourselves. It is the gift of a renewed community, in which we can find ourselves and discover our own renewal. It involves other's gifts, not only those common to human beings in the new creation but also those special gifts we have called charismata. All of these gifts, however, find their reason and justification in their use in the world to serve God—to serve God by serving our neighbors. If we have truly received our creation and new creation as the gift of God, there is no evading this life of service in the world—following the example of Jesus and empowered by the Spirit coming from him.

By using our gifts, the gifts of creation and the gifts of the new creation, in the struggle to overcome all forms of oppression holding any of God's people in bondage, whether political, economic, psychological, or intellectual, we make our response to the gift of the Spirit in Christ. That response is one of the most obvious ways God's presence can be made manifest in our world and one of the chief ways the power of God's new creation can be extended throughout the old.

God is not tied to the sacraments, but we are. When we live by the strength that comes from the Spirit through all the means of grace, we shall discover the full range of God's gifts to us. We shall also use those gifts to do God's work and manifest God's presence in the world.

5

Using the Gifts:
Ministry and
Mission

The work of Christians is the work of ministry, the same ministry God himself performed in and through Jesus Christ:

> Through Christ God reconciled us to himself and gave us the ministry of reconciliation; that is, God was in Christ reconciling the world to himself ... and entrusting to us the message of reconciliation.
>
> (2 Cor 5:18f)

Through this ministry of reconciliation the Church fulfills its mission, which is to restore all people to unity with God and each other in Christ (*BCP*, p. 855). Though the ministry of the Church is thus a single task with a single goal, it is possible to speak, as we have seen, of varieties of ministries, of different ways of serving God (1 Cor 12:4), which are directed at attaining the same single goal.[1] Any activity that contributes to building up the Christian community is properly called ministry (Eph 4:11f); the only distinctions have to do with the kind or scope of the activity.

In the Acts of the Apostles a distinction is drawn between the ministry or service of the Word and the serving of tables (Acts 6:2). These ministries were not absolutely separate even then, however, as is manifest from the fact that Stephen and Philip, who were among those specially chosen "to serve tables," proceeded almost at once to proclaim the Gospel even as the twelve disciples were doing (Acts 6:8-7:60; 8:5-13, 26-40).

The ministry called "serving tables" in the Book of Acts referred not only to the provision and distribution of food for those in special need, but also to the whole business of arranging common meals—a very important matter at a time when Christians of Jewish background hesitated or even refused to eat with Christians of Gentile background. The "service of tables" referred to in the New Testament thus adumbrates not only preparing food and waiting on tables at Church suppers, but also all those other ministries of practical love we now speak of as pastoral care and social service. In the same way, the New Testament "ministry of the Word" foreshadows not merely the exposition of the Gospel in the context of worship, but also the ministries of evangelism and education. The earliest Christian communities arose and grew up around these five ministries: worship, evangelism, education, pastoral care, and social service. These should not be thought of as separate, sharply defined areas of ministry that somehow exhaust the "varieties of service" of which Paul speaks (1 Cor 12:4), but as aspects of the one ministry of reconciliation Christ has committed to his Church. No one of these aspects can be neglected if the Church is to fulfill its total ministry.[2]

The various separate ministries comprehended within the Church's total ministry are shared and carried out by its ministers, among whom are lay persons, bishops, priests, and deacons. It will be useful to set out in full here the sections of the Catechism dealing with these ministers and their ministries (BCP, p.855f):

Q. What is the ministry of the laity?
A. The ministry of lay person is to represent Christ and his Church; to bear witness to him wherever they may be; and, according to the gifts given them, to carry on Christ's work of reconciliation in the world; and to take their place in the life, worship, and governance of the Church.

Q. What is the ministry of a bishop?

A. The ministry of a bishop is to represent Christ and his church, particularly as apostle, chief priest, and pastor of a diocese; to guard the faith, unity, and discipline of the whole church; to proclaim the Word of God; to act in Chirst's name for the reconciliation of the world and the building up of the Church; and to ordain others to continue Christ's ministry.

Q. What is the ministry of a priest or presbyter?

A. The ministry of a priest is to represent Christ and his Church, particularly as pastor to the people; to share with the bishop in the overseeing of the Church; to proclaim the Gospel; to administer the sacraments; and to bless and declare pardon in the name of God.

Q. What is the ministry of a deacon?

A. The ministry of a deacon is to represent Christ and his church, particularly as a servant of those in need; and to assist bishops and priests in the proclamation of the gospel and the administration of the sacraments.

Q. What is the duty of all Christians?

A. The duty of all Christians is to follow Christ; to come together week by week for corporate worship; and to work, pray, and give for the spread of the Kingdom of God.

If we read these passages carefully we shall see that the primary obligation of every minister is to represent Christ and his Church. Next we should observe that the special duties of bishops, priests, and deacons are additions to or elaborations of the duties of lay persons. This should not surprise us if we remember that the "higher" orders of ministry do not supersede the "lower," but include them. Thus every bishop is also a priest and a deacon, and every priest is also a deacon, and all are still lay persons. The laity is the name given to the people (*laos*) of God, and no one is excluded from the people of God merely because he or she has been ordained.

Thus the duty of lay persons to bear witness to Christ wherever they may be has its counterpart in the bishop's duty to proclaim the Word of God, the priest's duty to proclaim the gospel (which is the same thing), and the deacon's duty to assist bishops and priests in this proclamation. The lay person's obligation to take part in the life, worship, and governance of the church is spelled out for bishops, priests, and deacons in terms of specific responsibilities for guarding the faith, unity, and discipline of the Church, for exercising pastoral oversight, and for administering the sacraments.[3] The ministry of blessing and declaring God's forgiveness is reserved to priests and bishops, and that of ordaining others to continue Christ's ministry is reserved to bishops alone.

Only for lay persons and bishops is the duty of carrying on Christ's work of reconciliation explicitly set forth, but it clearly belongs also to the priests and deacons as representatives of Christ and his church. And as all Christians must fulfill their ministry "according to the gifts given them" so also are they enabled to fulfill their duty "to follow Christ; to come together week by week for corporate worship; and to work, pray, and give for the spread of the Kingdom of God."

Individual Christians may "specialize," so to speak, in one or another kind of ministry, but no Christian can refuse to minister, to serve, to the best of his or her ability, whenever a need for service arises. To be sure, the most appropriate and effective way of ministering to some people at some times will be to help them find a person better qualified than one's self to provide the specific service or minisry they need. This is not "passing the buck"; physicians frequently refer patients to specialists and also consult one another in difficult cases. Even Jesus' own disciples acted in this way: when they were unable to heal the epileptic boy themselves (Mk 9:14-19), they brought him to Jesus. We should never forget to do likewise, for no Christian has an "independent" ministry that is his or hers alone: each Christian shares in the ministry of the community to which he or she belongs—and in the ministry of the whole

Church, that is, in the ministry of the Lord Jesus Christ. The resources available for every Christian are, in the last analysis, unlimited.

Let us turn now to a discussion of the five areas or aspects of ministry we have mentioned above.

WORSHIP

Worship is the chief ministry required of Christians, and it overlaps all other ministries insofar as these contribute to the glorification of God: "Religion that is pure and genuine in the sight of God the Father will show itself by such things as visiting orphans and widows in their distress and keeping one's self uncontaminated by the world." (James 1:27, Phillips translation). [Note that the word translated "religion" here means specifically the worship of God as expressed in religious service or cult.]

Jesus did not neglect the regular cultic worship of his people: he attended the synagogue and taught there (Mk 1:21f, 39; 3:1; 6:2; Mt 9:35; Lk 4:15; 13:10), and his esteem for the Temple as a house of prayer is beyond question (Mk 11:17 and parallels). As a good Jew, Jesus probably observed the traditional times for personal prayer: thrice daily—at sunrise, at the time of the afternoon sacrifice, and at night before going to sleep.[4] We know that the night was a favorite time for him (cf. Mk 1:35; 6:46, 48; 14:17, 26, 32). Doubtless he intended his disciples to imitate him. He specially commends private prayer—"in secret" (Mt 6:6; cf. Lk 11:5—12)—and the prayer of two or more gathered in his name (Mt 18:19f). He encouraged the disciples to prayer boldly: "Whatever you ask in prayer, believe that you receive it, and you will" (Mk 11:24 Mt21:22), assuring them tha God will hear their prayers even as a father attends to the needs and wants of his children (Mt 7:7-11 Lk 11:9—13; cf. Mk 10:15). Most important of all, Jesus provided his disciples with a model for prayer—the Lord's Prayer—that continues to unite all Christians today (Mt 6:9-13 Lk 11:2-4).

The worship of the earliest Christian community in Jerusalem centered on the Temple (Acts 2:46; 3:1; 5:12; cf.

Lk 24:53, but other forms of worship, in private houses, are attested from the very beginning (Acts 2:46; 5:42; Rom 16:5; 1 Cor 16:19; Col 4:15; Phm 2). Various regular elements of this "house-worship" can be discerned.

Teaching

(Acts 2:42; 5:42; 11:26; 13:1; 1 Cor 14:26). The Scriptures of the Old Testament continued to be read as they had been before the separation from the synagogue, and sayings of Jesus (cf. 1 Cor 7:10, alluding to Mk 10:11ff; and Acts 20:35) and incidents from his life were no doubt recounted. Later on, the letters of St. Paul came to be read (1 5:27; Col 4:16; 2 Pet 3:15f). All of these were laid under tribute by the early Christians and applied to themselves and their new situations.[5]

Prophecy

Paul took it for granted that prophets might be present at the community's worship, and even took steps to regulate their participation (1Cor 14:26, 29-32). As we have seen, prophecy had the creative function of bringing new revelation to supplement and illuminate the tradition transmitted and interpreted by the teachers. The early Christians remained open to the possibility that the Spirit would speak with a living voice.

Prayer

(Acts 2:42; 6:4f; 12:5, 12; 13:3; 1 Cor 14:14f). Frequent use of the Lord's Prayer is proved by its development in divergent forms (Mt 6:9-13/Lk 11:2-4); its use is also probably attested by St. Paul's references to calling God "Abba, Father" (Rom 8:15; Gal 4:6). Prayer was also offered in more spontaneous fashion (Acts 4:24-30; 12:5, 12; 13:3). Pliny the Younger tells us that the early Christians "prayed to Jesus as to a god,"[6] and examples of such prayers can be found in the New Testament itself (Acts 7:59; 9:14, 21; 22:16; 1 Cor 16:22; 2 Cor 12:8).

Praise

Singing is mentioned explicitly by Luke (Acts 16:25) and Paul (1 Cor 14:15f; cf. Eph 5:19; Col 3:16), and actual examples of early hymns are preserved in such passages as the following:

Awake, O sleeper, and arise from the dead,
and Christ shall give you light.

(Eph 5:14)

Worthy art thou to take the scroll and to open its seals,
For thou wast slain and by thy blood didst ransom men for God
From every tribe and tongue and people and nation,
And hast made them a kingdom and priests to our God,
And they shall reign on earth.

. . .

Worthy is the Lamb who was slain,
To receive power and wealth and wisdom
and might and honor and glory and blessing!

. . .

To him who sits upon the throne and to the Lamb be blessing and
honor and glory and might for ever and ever!

(Rev 5:9f, 12, 13)[7]

The Lord's Supper

Only St. Paul uses this term (1 Cor 11:20), and he uses it as
Luke does the phrase "breaking of bread" (Acts 2:42, 46; 20:11;
cf. Lk 24:35) to refer not only to the sacramental blessing and
distribution of bread and wine but also to the whole common
meal of which this was originally a part.[8] The sacramental
blessing and distribution of bread and wine came very early to
be established as a separate rite and called *eucharistia* (thanksgiving); the common meal was continued as the *agape* (literally
"love," but in this technical use generally rendered as "love
feast") provided by Church members for fellowship and for
charity to the poor.[9] Our familiar term Eucharist is, obviously,
derived from *eucharistia*, and refers specifically to the Great
Thanksgiving over the bread and wine.

The significance of this rite for early Christians is evident
from the language used in speaking about it. It was a participation in the life and death of Christ ("in the blood . . . in the
body"—1 Cor 10:16); it was a reminder (*anamnesis*) of Jesus
Christ and all that he had done (1 Cor 11?24f). By proclaiming
the Lord's death "until he comes" (1 Cor 11:26), it struck a
triumphant note of eschatological hope. In sum, it was "a

testimony to the community's conintuing consciousness that its new covenant status depended on Jesus both for its inauguration and for its continuance."[10] The Holy Spirit was experienced as actively present in every part of Christian worship. Teaching and prophecy were recognized as charismata of the Spirit; the Spirit was felt as a helper of those "who do not know how to pray" as they ought (Rom 8:26), enabling them to cry, "Abba! Father!", and thus bearing witness to them that they are children and heirs of God (Rom 8:15-17; Gal 4:6f). Paul specifically says that he sings "with the Spirit" (1 Cor 14:15), and elsewhere we find mention of "spiritual" songs—songs prompted by and manifesting the Spirit (Eph 5:19; Col 3:16).[11] Finally, the bread and wine of the Eucharist are called spiritual food and drink—nourishment conveying the Spirit to those who partake of it (Didache 10:3; cf. 1 Cor 10:3).[12] This lively awareness of the presence and power of God's Spirit among them was the cause of the joyful exuberance characteristic of the community life and worship of the first Christians (Acts 2:46; 1 Pet 1:6, 8).[13]

The ministry of worship, which is the privilege and responsibility of all Christians, has been and remains of importance because it gives a sense of identity, a sense of belonging, a sense of interdependence, to those who take part in it. Corporate worship, especially, has never been more important for Christians than it is today for we who live in a time of great emphasis on the individual, on the self.[14] The present generation has with good cause been called the "me" generation; we are urged on every side to gratify our selfish desires, to "realize" our *selves*, to incorporate everything, as it were, into our lives, to consider every other person as our satellite. But we cannot "realize" ourselves without God, who alone is truly real, who is both center and boundary of all existence, and who wishes to incorporate us into his people. When Christians come together for worship they engage in a "corporate act that transcends both time and space"[15] and makes those who participate in it aware of their fellowship in the one Spirit (2 Cor 13:14; cf. Phil 2:1) not only with other members of their own congregation, but with all Christians in every place in every age. Worship also makes Christians mindful of their continuing dependence on Jesus Christ whose commands they obey when they unite in the Lord's Prayer and the Lord's Supper. Finally, since worship, understood in its broadest and deepest sense (cf. Mt 25:31-45; James 1:27; Rom 12:1), involves the totality of a Christian's relationships, it reminds us that all life is to be lived in dependence on God.

EDUCATION AND EVANGELISM

The other four ministries may be grouped into two pairs: (1) education and pastoral care, ministries that are exercised primarily within the Christian community, and (2) evangelism and social service, ministries that are exercised primarily by the Christian community for the benefit of those outside it. This is only a rough-and-ready classification, of course, as all rigid classifications of Christain ministries must be, since these ministries overlap and shade off into one another—being, as we have often emphasized, all only varieties of the single ministry of reconciliation. Thus Christian education, which—as we have said—is the transmission and reinterpretation of tradition accepted by the church as in some way authoritative (e.g., the scriptures of the Old and New Testaments and later saints' and scholars' teachings, which have been tested in the crucible of the Church's experience), cannot be sharply distinguished from evangelism, which, in the strict sense, means the proclamation of the Gospel to those who have not heard it before. There are a great many people who would be counted—and who would, indeed, count themselves—as within the Church, but who still need and welcome a clearer presentation of the Gospel in terms that will enable them to attain a better understanding of it for the sake of their own ministries of teaching and evangelism. On the other hand, there are a great many people who would be considered—and who consider themselves—to be outside the Church, but who need and welcome some knowledge of Christian tradition and history before they can really hear, with understanding, the Gospel from which Christian tradition ultimately derives and apart from which Christian history seems mere trivial marginalia on the history of the "real" world.

Christian education is, in any event, concerned with more than the transmission of Christian tradition, because it has, or should have, the function of broadening Christians' knowledge of "the vital issues of the day, such as peace, racism, human rights, sexism, ecology—to name but a few."[16]

Similarly, every Christian needs to understand the ministry of evangelism, since all Christians, lay or ordained, have the obligation to bear witness to Jesus Christ wherever they may be (BCP, p. 855). Even Christians who do not preach the Gospel in words do preach it—or fail to preach it—in their lives, and their behavior may affect the attitude of outsiders toward the Gospel far more profoundly, for good or for ill, than any spoken or written exposition of it. St. Paul warns the Roman Christians that the name of God is blasphemed among the Gentiles because of their behavior (Rom 2:24, quoting Isaiah 52:5), while, on the other hand, Tertullian tells us that pagans were attracted by the behavior of the Christians among them, saying, "See how these Christians love one another!"[17] Thus the responsibility for evangelism rests on the whole membership of each Christian community, not merely on its ordained members; and this responsibility must be recognized and accepted—consciously and willingly—by each member for himself or herself. Christians should find joy in their work for Christ's sake as well as for their own and should be aware of how their profession, trade, or occupation contributes to or detracts from justice and equity in society.

Furthermore, though an old familiar saying has it that "actions speak louder than words," an equally wise saying runs, "the word without the deed is empty, but the deed without the word is dumb." It is surely important for Christians to proclaim the Gospel in their lives by their behavior, and in some societies this is all that Christians are permitted by the secular authorities to do. But this is not the case in our society, and so Christians who live here have no excuse for failing to proclaim the Gospel by word as well as by deed; they must and do so boldly. In our conversations with non-Christians, are we ashamed to refer explicitly to the faith that conditions our decisions and our actions? When we speak of the interplay of forces in our private and public lives, do we hesitate to name the Lord of history as well, and do we hesitate to acknowledge him explicitly as our Lord? Christians should remember that words of St. Paul: "I am not ashamed of the Gospel: it is the power of God for salvation" (Rom 1:16); and also the words of Jesus: "Everyone who publicly acknowledges me I shall acknowledge in the presence of my Father in Heaven, but whoever publicly disowns me I shall disown before my Father in Heaven" (Mt 10:32f, adapted from Phillips' translation; cf. Lk 12:8f).

PASTORAL CARE AND SOCIAL SERVICE

Pastoral care and social service, again, are also two sides of one coin: the former is directed primarily inward to the Christian community and its members, the latter primarily outward to the larger society of which the Christian congregation is a part. These ministries also belong to the whole membership of a Christian community, not merely to its professional leaders. It is, of course, true that "the particular gifts and talents of those who have special vocational callings and who have special training in pastoral care must be recognized and used,"[18] but this does not mean that other members of the community are released from the obligation to meet together "to encourage one another to love and do good deeds... [and] to help one another's faith" (Heb 10:24f, Phillips). One of the meanings of community is "common possession or participation," and though we know from Acts 4:32 that in the early Church this was extended to material possessions and money, it is most important to understand that it means a total sharing of each individual's faith and hope and love as well as each one's fears and troubles. Christians are to share one another's faith, to help one another with the same help they have received from God (2 Cor 1:3f), and to bear one another's burdens (Gal 6:2).

The members of a congregation who share one another's faith and bear one another's burdens will soon find the strength to reach beyond the boundaries of their own communities to meet the needs of those who live on its fringes or altogether outside of it. The motivation for Christian service to non-Christian society is found in the commandment, "You shall love your neighbor as yourself,"[19] as this is interpreted in the Parable of the Good Samaritan (Lk 10:30-37) and infinitely extended in the Sermon on the Mount: "But I say to you, 'Love your enemies' " (Mt 5:44; Lk 6:27). The Christian "neighborhood" is not a ghetto: it is open both from within and from without; Christ has broken down all dividing walls (Eph 2:14).

Christians are, therefore, called to ministry, to service, wherever human beings are in need.[20] Some human "needs can be expressed simply in terms of money (food, clothing, housing, consumption goods), some less easily (social adjustment, free access to cultural life and religious engagement, political emancipation, recognition of human dignity in all areas of life."[21] Every human need summons Christians to service. The magnitude of the tasks that confront Christians, the scope of the ministries they are called to perform, would indeed be daunting were it not for the fact that it is God who equips us to perform them.

> As each of you has received a gift, use it in serving one another, as faithful stewards of the many-splendored grace of God. Is yours a gift of utterance? Then speak as one who proclaims the oracles of God. Is yours a gift of ministry? Use it in the strength which God supplies. In everything you do let God be glorified through Jesus Christ, to whom belong all praise and dominion for ever and ever. Amen.
>
> (1 Pet 4:10f)

NOTES

Abbreviations used in the text and footnotes:

BCP = *The Book of Common Prayer* (New York: The Church Hymnal Corporation, 1979).

IDB = *The Interpreter's Dictionary of the Bible* (Nashville: Abington Press, vols. 1—4, 1962ff; Supplementary volume, 1976).

TDNT = *Theological Dictionary of the New Testamant* (Grand Rapids: Wm. B. Eerdmans Publishing Company, 1964—76), vols. 1—10; ed. by Gerhard Kittel, trans. by Geoffrey W. Bromiley.

Chapter 1. The Church Moves Toward Renewal

1. Charles Williams has done something very close to this in *The Descent of the Dove* (New York: Oxford University Press, 1939).

2. Charles Henry Brent, *Things that Matter*, ed. Frederick W. Kates (New York: Harper & Bros., 1949), 42.

3. Cf., e.g., Alfred T. Hennelly, *Theologies in Conflict: The Challenge of Juan Luis Segundo* (Maryknoll, N.Y.: Orbis Books, 1979), passim.

4. Cf. infra, Chapter 3.

5. Philo, *Posterity and Exile of Cain*, 42; *Confusion of Tongues*, 123, 127. Philo's word for gift is *charis* (cf. infra, p. 29).

6. Cf. infra, p. 30.

7. Bernard Haldane, *Good Experiences: Study Guide to Gifts for Ministry* (Washington, D.C., 1980), 1.

8. W. J. Hollenweger, *The Pentecostals* (Augsburg, 1972). Cf. also Richard F. Lovelace, *Dynamics of Spiritual Life* (Downers Grove, Ill.: Inter-Varsity Press, 1980), 133.

Chapter 2. The Gifts of God in Creation

1. *Oxford Dictionary of the Christian Church*, 2d edition, s.v. "Seven Gifts of the Spirit" and infra, chap. 3, note 16.

2. St. Augustine, *The Trinity* in vol. 45 of *The Fathers of the Church* (Washington, D.C.: Catholic University of America Press, 1963) trans. by Stephen McKenna, C.SS.R., 45:266.

3. Søren Kierkegaard, *The Sickness unto Death*, trans. Walter Lowrie (Princeton, 1946).

Chapter 3. The Gifts of God in the New Creation, Part One

1. The Old Testament says nothing about the divine image being lost, but the loss is taken for granted by Paul who speaks of the restoration of the image (Rom 8:29; 1 Cor 15:49; 2 Cor 3:18, cf. Col 3:10).

2. The word *charisma* is not certainly attested in pre-Pauline literature. It probably is not an actual coinage of Paul, however, since it does occur in the writings of the sophist Alciphron (second centry A.D.), who is hardly likely to have been influenced by any specially Christian vocabulary. (Ulrich Brockhaus, *Charisma und Amt* [Wuppertal: Theologischer Verlag Rolf Brockhaus, 1972], 129; cf. Hans Conzelmann, *TDNT* 9:402f.)

3. "Spiritual" (*pneumatikon*) is in the Greek of Rom 1:11, however; RSV has "blessing" for charisma in 2 Cor 1:11, elsewhere simply "gift."

4. *Charis* is itself occasionally translated by "gift" in English versions of the Bible (1 Cor 16:3: RSV, Phillips, NEB, TEV; 2 Cor 8:4: KJV, Phillips; in both passages it refers to the "thank-offering" Paul was collecting for the "saints" in Jerusalem).

5. Cf. H. Conzelmann in *TDNT*, esp. 9:394.

6. James D. G. Dunn, *Jesus and the Spirit* (Philadelphia: Westminster Press, 1975), 205.

7. It is worth noting, however, that James Moffatt, whose scholarship and opinions on biblical translation still deserve respect, did not hesitate to use "talent" for charisma in Rom 12:6 and 1 Cor 12:4 in *The Bible: A New Translation* (1922).

8. We have preferred to speak of "extraordinary" gifts as contrasted with "innate" or "inherent" ones. It is difficult to maintain an absolute distinction: musical talent, for example, is presumably innate, but in the child Mozart it was surely extraordinary.

9. Cf. the typologies discussed by Enrique Dussell in his essay, "The Differentiation of Charisms," in Christian Duquoc and Casiano Floristan, *Charisms in the Church* (New York: Seabury Press, 1978), 38—55.

10. Conzelmann, *TDNT* 9:404.

11. Ibid.

12. This triad (twice in 1 Cor 12:28f) occurs nowhere else in the undisputed epistles; however, the combination of "apostles" with "prophets" and/or "teachers" or of the last two with each other is found frequently in other early Christian literature. The full triad occurs in Eph 4:11, with "evangelists" and "pastors" interpolated before "teachers"; "apostles and prophets" occurs in Eph 2:20; 3:5; Rev 18:20; and Didache 11:3; "apostles and teachers" appears in 2 Tim 1:11; Hermas Sim IX 15, 4; 16, 5; 25, 2, and Hermas Vis III 5, 1; finally, "prophets and teachers" is found in Acts 13:1. The passages in Ephesians and 2 Timothy are certainly dependent upon Paul, and the others may be also.

13. Rudolf Bultmann, *TDNT* 6:217f.

14. Dunn, *Jesus and the Spirit*, 211. Bultmann (*TDNT* 6:219) says without explanation that faith "is not a gift of the spirit."

15. Bultmann, indeed, says that it is impossible to do so (*TDNT* 1:708, n. 73).

16. Archibald Robertson and Alfred Plummer, *A Critical and Exegetical Commentary on the First Epistle of St. Paul to the Corinthians*, 2d ed. (Edinburgh: T. & T. Clark, 1914), 265. It is true that both wisdom and knowledge are listed among the traditional "seven gifts of the Holy Spirit" (cf. *Oxford Dictionary of the*

Christian Church, in loc.), but the scriptural passage from which this list derives (Isaiah 11:2) speaks rather of the Spirit of the Lord promised to the Davidic Messiah: "the spirit of wisdom and understanding, the spirit of counsel and might, the spirit of knowledge and the fear of the Lord." (the seventh of these so-called gifts, piety, is mentioned only in the Vulgate.) Cf. supra, chapter 2.

17.   Ulrich Wilckens (*TDNT* 7:522) points out that Paul is not here denying the possibility of preaching the Gospel in the language of Greek philosophy.

18.   Cf. Bultmann, *TDNT* 1:707.

19.   Dunn, *Jesus and the Spirit*, 237. The same distinction is made by Gerhard Friedrich (*TDNT* 6:85), but is questioned by E. E. Ellis (*IDB* Supp., 701).

20.   For examples we may mention (1) many of the sayings of Jesus himself, who taught with authority and wisdom (Mk 1:22; 6:2); the prediction of Agabus in Acts 11:27f; (3) Paul's pronouncements in 1 Cor 7:25—40 (note the final sentence: "I think I have the Spirit of God") and in 1 Cor 15:51 ("Lo! I tell you a mystery"); (4) the teaching of a prophet or circle of prophets may be reflected in the "faithful sayings" of the Pastoral Epistles (1 Tim 1:15; 3:1; 4:8f; 2 Tim 2:11-13; Tit 3:3-8); (5) the whole Book of Revelation is an example of Christian prophecy (cf. 1:3; 22:7, 10, 18f). "though cast in an apocalyptic form, it is the proclamation of a man 'in the Spirit' who expounds from the imagery of the Old Testament the new revelation of God's victory in Christ and in those who belong to Christ." (M. H. Shepherd, Jr., "Prophet in the New Testament," *IDB* 3:919f; cf. also E. E. Ellis, "Prophecy in the Early Church," *IDB* Supp., 701.)

21.   Dunn, *Jesus and the Spirit*, 243.

22.   Paul thus differs from Luke, who in Acts 2:6 is plainly speaking of human languages.

23.   Dunn, *Jesus and the Spirit*, 231. In an effort to understand 1 Cor 14:21-25 differently, J. B. Phillips has here departed form the accepted Greek text and translates v. 22 thus: "... 'tongues' are a sign of God's power, not for those who are unbelievers but for those who already believe." There is, however, no textual support of any kind for Phillips' conjecture; he says only that "he felt bound to conclude, from the

sense of the next three verses, that we have here either a slip of the pen on the part of Paul, or, more probably, a copyist's error" (footnote in Phillips' translation, in loc.). However, no other commentators—ancient or modern—have felt the need to emend the text in this fashion; Dunn's interpretation agrees with that of the majority of scholars.

24. W. J. Samarin, *Tongues of Men and Angels* (New York: the Macmillan Company, 1972), 42.

25. Dunn, *Jesus and the Spirit*, 253.

26. The word is Samarin's. He writes:

> The initial experience of speaking in tongues comes in many ways. One is immediate and fluent.... Others acquire glossolalia gradually.... There are those who experience an unconscious switch from their normal language (say English) to glossolalia.... In some people glossolalia appears first as a form of "inner speech." (pp. 162f)

27. Samarin shows conclusively, however (in the present writer's opinion), that glossolalia is not a language (Samarin, *Tongues of Men and Angels*; chs. 4-6, passim).

28. Ibid., 197-202.

29. Ibid. 202-205, 210f.

30. Ibid., 209.

31. Ibid., 215.

32. Ibid., 163.

33. Ibid.

34. Ibid., 166.

35. Ibid., 165, referring to Harold Horton, *The Gifts of the Spirit* (London: Assemblies of God Publishing House, 1966), 73.

36. Dunn, *Jesus and the Spirit*, 248.

37. Ibid., 425, n. 255.

38. The following table illustrates the shift of preference:

		KJV	RSV
diakonos	= servant	7	17
	= minister (noun)	20	7
diakonia	= service	2	8
	= ministry	16	12
diakoneō	= serve	9	19
	= minister (verb)	22	5

(Corresponding totals do not agree because these renderings do not exhaust those used in either version.)

39. The distinction between *serve* and *minister* (verb) is instructive: one *serves* a person who is richer or more powerful than one's self, but one *ministers* to the poor and helpless.

40. Plato, *Gorgias* 492b, quoted by Hermann W. Beyer, *TDNT* 2:82.

41. *Gorgias*, 505a, quoted by Beyer, ibid., 83. The Greeks did not think serving was improper for women: "We have harlots for our pleasure, concubines for our daily physical use, wives to bring up legitimate children and to be faithful stewards in household matters" (Pseudo-Demosthenes, *Against Neaira*, 59, 122; quoted by Albrecht Oepke in *TDNT* 1:778). Plato's arguments in favor of equality for women (*Republic* 5:5-8) fell on deaf ears.

42. Beyer, *TDNT* 2:82.

43. Ibid., 86.

44. Beyer, *TDNT* 3:1036.

45. There is some difference of opinion about the meaning of *proistamenos*. The verb with which it is connected (*proistanai*) is used in 1 Th 5:12 and 1 Tim 5:17 of presiding over the congregation, and in 1 Tim 3:4, 5, 12 of managing one's own household. This meaning is reflected in the renderings of Rom 12:8 that appear in *KJV* ("he that ruleth"), Phillips ("the man that wields authority"), and *NEB* ("a leader"). But *proistanai* can also mean "be concerned about, care for, give aid:" some scholars (e.g., Dobschütz, against Harnack) prefer this meaning in 1 Th 5:12, and *RSV* adopts it in Rom 12:8 ("he who gives aid"). The idea of caring concern hardly seems incompatible with that of guiding or presiding, however, which is surely the primary meaning (cf. C.E.B. Cranfield, *A Critical and Exegetical Commentary on the Epistle to the Romans*, Edinburgh: T. & T. Clark, 1979, 2:625-27).

46. Beyer, *TDNT*, 3:1036.

47. Quoted by Cranfield, *Critical and Exegetical Commentary*, 627.

48. Dunn, *Jesus and the Spirit*, 211.

49. Ibid., 210f.

50. Cf. A. Oepke in *TDNT* 3:199.

51. Cf. also Gen 10:17f; Ex 15:26; Hos 6:1; 7:1; 11:3; and many Psalms.

52. Werner Foerster in *TDNT* 7:990.
53. Cf. also 1 Cor 1:21; 2 Tim 1:9; Rom 3:26, 30; 4:5; 8:30, 33.
54. Brockhaus, *Charisma und Amt*, 237.
55. Ibid., 237f.
56. Jesus is called apostle in Heb 3:1; he is called prophet (twelve times) and teacher (forty-one times) in the Gospels.
57. Dunn, *Jesus and the Spirit*, 281.
58. Didache 11:7-11 gives instructions for detecting such impostors, while insisting on proper respect for genuine prophets. Lucian of Samosata (b. ca. 120 A.D., d. after 180) gives, from an intellectual pagan's point of view, an amusing account of a false prophet imposing on the charity of credulous Christians in *The Passing of Peregrinus* (Loeb Classical Library, Lucian, vol. 5).
59. Didache 11:1f warns against teachers who do not transmit the tradition faithfully.
60. The name of the apostle in Rom 16:7 may be read either as *Junia* (feminine) or *Junias* (masculine); however, "Junias" as a name is otherwise unknown. Ancient commentators took Andronicus and Junia to be husband and wife (Walter Bauer, *A Greek-English Lexicon of the New Testament and Other Early Christian Literature*, 2d American edition, s.v. Iounias). It is not clear from the context whether Andronicus and Junia(s) were apostles of Christ or only delegates of Churches.
61. Brockhaus, *Charisma und Amt*, 97.
62. Dunn, *Jesus and the Spirit*, 273f. According to G. Friedrich (*TDNT* 6:854), apostles were replaced by evangelists.
63. Friedrich, *TDNT* 6:850.
64. We have already given examples of Paul's charismatic teaching supra, p. 36).
65. Beyer, *TDNT* 3:1036.
66. Dunn, *Jesus and the Spirit*, 74ff.
67. Among these may be mentioned Simon Magus (Acts 8:9) and Apollonius of Tyana (Philostratus, *Life of Apollonius of Tyana* (Loeb Classical Library; London: William Heinemann Ltd., 1948.
68. 2 Cor 11:13.
69. Mt 7:15; 24:11, 24 = Mk 13:22; Lk 6:26; Acts 13:6; 16:6; 2 Pet 2:1; 1 Jn 4:1; Rev 16:13; 19:20; 20:10.

70.   2 Pet. 2:1.

71.   Hitler and Mussolini are among the most notorious, but many minor "false prophets" might be mentioned, such as the Rev. Jim Jones whose followers unquestioningly drank poison at his behest.

72.   *Oxford Classical Dictionary*, 2d edition, 129f (s.v. Asclepius).

73.   Philostratus, *Life of Apollonius*, 1:317, 319, 457.

74.   Tacitus, *Histories*, 4:81; Suetonius, *Vespasian*, 7: Dio Cassius, 65:8. Tacitus and Suetonius say Vespasian used spittle to cure a blind man, as Jesus did according to Mk 8:23 and Jn 9:6. The use of spittle to heal was a "widespread Jewish practice" (J. A. Wharton, "Spit," in *IBD* 4:437).

75.   Mesmer gave his name to "mesmerism," now called hypnotism; Quimby was a forerunner and mentor of Mary Baker Eddy. (Cf. Frank Podmore, *Mesmerism and Christian Science* [Philadelphia: G. W. Jacobs and Co., 1909], passim.)

76.   In the New Testament itself we find Simon Magus (Acts 8:9) and Elymas (Acts 13:8); we have already mentioned Apollonius of Tyana (supra, notes 64 and 70; he was said to have been miraculously translated from Smyrna to Ephesus; cf. Philostratus, *Life of Apollonius* 1:365.

77.   The medium D.D. Home (1833-86) demonstrated his mastery of self-levitation before "unimpeachable" witnesses; he was the only medium to produce such physical phenomena who was never detected in deception (J. H. Leuba, *Encyclopedia of Religion and Ethics* (Edinburgh: T. & T. Clark, 1909) 10:451b). The powers of the "psychic" Uri Geller are still under investigation as this is being written (cf. Adam Smith [pseud.], *Powers of Mind* [New York: Random House, 1975]).

78.   David Christie-Murray, *Voices from the Gods* (London: Routledge and Kegan Paul, 1978), passim.

79.   Samarin, *Tongues of Men and Angels*, 76, 98.

80.   Cf. Sidney Cohen, M.D., *The Beyond Within* (New York: Atheneum, 1965), passim.

81.   Jacques Guillet, S.J., *Discernment of Spirits* (Collegeville, Minn.: The Liturgical Press, 1957), 43.

82. Cf. supra, 31f.

83. Cf., e.g., Origen: "No one can possess any divine charisma unless it is given from heaven." (*Frag. 44 in Joannem.*) for other citations see G.W.H. Lampe, *A Patristic Greek Lexicon* (Oxford, 1961ff), 1518, s.v. *charisma*, A, a-d.

84. Cf. Lampe, *Greek Lexicon*, F2, G1.

85. The citations given by Lampe include faith, prophecy, gifts of healings, miracles, chastity, almsgiving, eloquence, the forgiveness of sins, discernment of spirits, and Christian vocation as such. One charisma less obviously related to the Pauline ones is the gift of tears (Athanasius, *De Virginitate*, 17).

86. The Apostolic Constitutions (8.1.8,9) adjures Christians not to praise those who receive charismata above those who do not, and Gregory of Nazianzus (*Orationes* 8.15) observes that it is not the practice of the saints to glory in charsimata.

87. This "institutionalization" of charismata is reflected in the writings of the Fathers from the earliest period. Ignatius (*Smyrn. proem.*) says that the Church has been favored with every gift. Irenaeus (*Against Heresies* 3.32.4) says "it is not possible to number the gifts which the Church has received from God throughout the whole world . . . and makes use of every day for the benefit of the nations," and he adds (4.26.2) that these gifts are given through the episcopal office. Epiphanius explicitly calls priesthood a charisma, and many Fathers refer to the transmission of this gift by the laying on of hands (cf. Lampe, *Greek Lexicon*, E).

88. Origen, *Frag. 44 in Joannem.*

89. Leontius of Jerusalem, *Against the Monophysites.*

90. Lovelace, 125f.

91. Ibid., 127.

92. Ibid., 262ff.

93. Ibid., 133.

Chapter 4. The Gifts of God in the New Creation, Part Two.

1. James D. G. Dunn's *Jesus and the Spirit* is a near approach to this. (Its subtitle is "A Study of the Religious Charismatic Experience of Jesus and the First Christians as Reflected in the New Testament.")

2. *History of Israel's Religion, The Interpreter's Bible* (Nashville: Abington Press, 1952), esp. 1:344.

3. Edward Schillebeeckx, *Jesus* (Seabury, 1979), 391.

4. Paul Tillich, *Systematic Theology* (University of Chicago Press, 1957), 2:119ff.

5. Paul does not call love a charisma, but a "fruit" of the Spirit (Gal 5:22).

6. In *Luthers Werke: Die Deutsche Bibel* 7:3 (Weimar Edition).

7. Baptism is called a charisma by Clement of Alexandria (*Paedagogus* I.6); the Eucharist is called a charisma in Acts of Thomas A.51. Origen says that baptism is "the beginning and source of divine charismata." (*In Joannem 6.33*).

8. Cf. supra, discussion of *charis* in chap. 3.

9. Peter Lombard, *Sentences*, IV, 1.5.

10. Strictly speaking, of course, God's forgiveness is prior: God exercises his freedom to forgive, we are given freedom to accept or reject. Note how in the story of the paralytic let down through the roof (Mk 2:1-12 and parallels) Jesus forgives the man's sins without asking for repentance.

11. Cf. supra, Charismata of Healing, p. 43-46.

12. Tillich, *The Courage to Be* (New Haven: Yale University Press, 1952).

13. Cf. James D. G. Dunn, *Baptism in the Holy Spirit* (London: SCM Press, 1970), 228.

14. *Summa Theologica*, 3a, 65, 4.

15. Cf. supra, note 7.

16. Cf., e.g., Gregory Dix, *The Shape of the Liturgy*, Westminster, 1944; and Joachim Jeremias, *The Eucharistic Words of Jesus*, trans. Norman Perrin from the third German edition, 1966.

17. Scholars are divided on this question. Jeremias thinks the Last Supper was a Passover, but gives a list of scholars who do not share his view.

18. Cf. supra, note 7.

Chapter 5. Using the Gifts: Ministry and Mission

1. Cf. supra, Chapter Three, pp. 42f.

2. Herbert T. Mayer makes this abundantly clear in his

book, *Pastoral Care: Its Roots and Renewal.* He speaks of five "functions" or tasks around which Christian communities developed. These "functions" do not correspond exactly to what we have called "aspects" of ministry, but they overlap:

> The first function was...sharing with...other members...those material and spiritual gifts and problems that God had given each member. The second function was that of worshiping the triune God. The third function was that of serving one another and the world in physical and spiritual matters. The fourth function was that of nurturing and building one another up. The fifth function was that of seeking to share with unbelievers the great gifts and experiences that they shared with each other in Jesus Christ. There is no suggestion in the New Testament that one of these functions is more important than another. Rather, the picture that the New Testament presents is that all five must go on constantly and will go on side by side in a well ordered Christian *koinonia* [community], (pp. 30f).

3. The laity assist in the administration of the sacraments, not only because they may be licensed to administer the Cup, but simply because they are present.

4. Joachim Jeremias, *The Prayers of Jesus* (SCM Press, 1967), 75.

5. Dunn, *Jesus and the Spirit*, 186.

6. Pliny the Younger, *Letter to Trajan* (*Epistles* 10. 96, 97).

7. To these could be added other hymns from the Apocalypse (e.g., Rev 4:8, 11; 7:10, 12, 15-17; 11:17f; 15:3f; 19:1-3, 5, 6-8). The poems in the Lucan Infancy Narratives came very early to be used in Christian worship (Magnificat, Lk 1:46-55; Benedictus, Lk 1:68-79; Gloria in Excelsis, Lk 2:14; and Nunc Dimittis, Lk 2:29-32), and many scholars believe that at least some of the great Christological passages (Jn 1:1-5; Phil 2:5-11; Col 1:15-20; 1 Tim 3:16) are, or are based on, early hymns. Older scholars, especially, were fond of referring to 1 Cor 13 as a "hymn" or "psalm" in praise of love (so Robertson and Plummer, 285), but since it forms an integral part of Paul's argument about spiritual gifts, this is now disputed. It may certainly be regarded as an example of inspired utterance, however.

8. The "words of institution" as they are preserved in 1 Cor 11:24-26 clearly indicate this: first the bread is broken (v. 24), and then after supper the cup is distributed (v. 25.)

9.   For details see the articles *Agape* and *Lord's Supper* in the *Interpreter's Dictionary of the Bible*.

10.   Dunn, *Jesus and the Spirit*, 185.

11.   Ibid., 238.

12.   In 1 Cor 10:3 Paul is speaking of an Old Testament pre-figuration of the Eucharist (cf. H. Conzelmann, *First Corinthians* [Philadelpis: Fortress Press, 1976] 166). The practice of invoking the Holy Spirit in the consecration of the bread and wine came much later (Hans Lietzmann, *Mass and Lord's Supper* [Leiden: E. J. Brill, 1979], xiv, and chap. 4 and 8).

13.   Dunn, *Jesus and the Spirit*, 188.

14.   Cf. supra, chap. 2

15.   John M. Allin, "A Proposal to Every Congregation," in *The Next Step in Mission* (New York: Office of Communication, The Episcopal Church Center, 1982), 7.

16.   Ibid.

17.   Tertullian, *Apology,*. in *The Fathers of the Church*, (New York: Fathers of the Church, Inc., 1950) trans. by Sr. Emily J. Daly, C.S.J., 10:99.

18.   Mayer, *Pastoral Care*, 44.

19.   Lev 19:18, quoted in Mt 5:43; 19:19; 22:39; Mk 12:31, 33; Lk 10:27; Rom 12:10; 13:9; Gal 5:14; James 2:8.

20.   Adrian M. van Peski, *The Outreach of Diakonia* (Assen: Van Gorcum & Comp., N.V., 1968), 131.

21.   Ibid., 133.

INDEX

104 / Index